# Bushcraft for Kids

*Mastering the Art of Outdoor Survival
and Thriving in the Wilderness*

# Table of Contents

# Introduction Letter to Parents

While encouraging children to venture outdoors is essential for their health and well-being, it's natural for parents to be concerned for their safety. It's paramount for children to understand the importance of safety, practical skills to use in the wilderness, and the steps to take in challenging situations. This book is not just about knowing practical skills – it's about using them effectively in the natural world, preparing the child for outdoor exploration.

The purpose of this book extends far beyond teaching outdoor skills. It is a practical guide for your child, nurturing a genuine passion for the great outdoors and creating a connection with nature.

**Love for Learning:** Through simple explanations, the book aims to ignite a love for learning. Your child will discover the skills of observation, exploration, and discovery to use in the natural world, sparking curiosity and a thirst for knowledge.

**Building Confidence:** Your child will gain confidence in their abilities by mastering practical skills. This newfound self-assurance can positively impact their overall development and sense of independence.

**Environmental Stewardship:** The book educates children about the value of nature, the significance of wildlife preservation, and the necessity of keeping the habitat unaffected during their explorations.

**Family Bonding:** As a parent, you can join your children in these outdoor adventures. The book provides a fantastic opportunity for quality family time, strengthening the parent-child bond and creating cherished memories.

**Safety First:** Rest assured, the book places utmost importance on safety. Your child will learn essential skills such as first aid, safely foraging food, navigation, and emergency preparedness, ensuring they are well-equipped to handle various outdoor situations responsibly.

The potential risks of nature are unpredictable, which is precisely why extensive safety guidelines and easy-to-understand steps are shared throughout the book. Your child's safety is the utmost priority. This journey will enrich your child's life and create lasting memories and a strong sense of environmental responsibility.

Thank you for entrusting the book with the opportunity to inspire a new generation of responsible and nature-loving explorers.

# Introduction Letter to Children

Get ready for a thrilling journey into bushcraft and outdoor survival that gives you life skills that can be used during challenging situations in the wild. The book is more than just words and pages! It takes you to a world where you become the ultimate adventurer while keeping yourself and those around you safe. The journey is not about reading or cramming in information. Instead, it's about doing, experiencing, and embracing the wild while thriving in every situation.

As you read through its pages, you'll discover how to build a shelter, make a fire, find your way in the wilderness, and so much more. These are the skills of true adventurers, skills that empower you to explore the world around you. However, remember that these skills must be used. The more you use them, the more valuable they become. Besides providing an overview of these essential survival skills, you'll be introduced to the basics of foraging food in the wilderness and first aid techniques to face any extreme survival situation with knowledge and confidence.

The wilderness is not just a place to survive. It's also a place to thrive. It's where you'll discover the wonders of nature and the hidden life under every rock. Nature is your teacher, and this book is your guide. You'll learn to venture outdoors, explore the secrets of the woods, climb the peaks, and run along the shorelines. Feel the wind on your face, listen to the songs of the birds, and watch the dance of the trees. Nature is a treasure trove of experiences waiting for you.

Keep this book as your companion because each page will be a stepping stone on your path toward becoming a true explorer. Share your stories with loved ones, see your discoveries, and share your adventures. The wilderness is your playground, and you are its cherished guest. Wishing you an incredible journey.

# Section 1: What Is Bushcraft?

Do you love venturing into great outdoor adventures? If yes, you need to learn a set of important wilderness survival skills for your safety and enjoyment to make the most of your outdoor adventure. These survival skills are called bushcraft or survival skills. You need bushcraft skills to live in wild, remote areas or a place that does not have much habitation.

Camping is all about enjoying the natural environment and fun activities. In contrast, *bushcraft* consists of a wide range of practical knowledge and expertise needed to survive and thrive in the wild. Bushcraft includes building a shelter, making a fire, and foraging for food and water. It teaches you how to rely on yourself, become adaptable, live in the wild with minimal resources, and stay prepared for anything to come. In this section, you will learn all about bushcraft and the outdoor skills that every little adventurer must learn.

**Bushcraft includes building a shelter, making a fire, and foraging for food and water.**

# Cultural and Historical Importance

Bushcraft or outdoor skills have had great cultural and historical significance throughout various periods and civilizations. People have relied on these skills to survive in nature throughout history. From ancient foraging or hunter-gatherer communities to modern-day civilizations, these skills, including starting a fire, building a shelter, foraging, and the ability to navigate, have always been essential for survival.

These outdoor skills are still quite prominent in many indigenous cultures and are deep-rooted in their way of life. This knowledge is passed down through the generations to preserve traditional techniques and apprehensions. Moreover, this know-how is heavily tied to cultural practices and rituals that reflect the powerful connection between nature and mankind. Bushcraft has also played a huge role in many explorations and historical events. Wilderness skills were extremely important for the survival and success of the early explorers who ventured into new territories and the discoverers who settled into the new lands. These capabilities helped them adapt to new environments, face challenges, and establish developed communities.

Today, bushcraft still holds cultural significance as it fosters resilience, adaptability, self-reliance, and a deep love of nature. It helps you reconnect to your ancestral roots by understanding the elemental skills that equipped your forefathers to survive in the wilderness. Moreover, these skills have become more prominent with the advancement of technology to help you disconnect from the modern world and embrace a simple and sustainable lifestyle. Learning about bushcraft will not only equip you with the ability to survive in the wild, but it will also help you to create a deeper connection with nature, boost self-confidence, and provide a sense of empowerment.

# Why Should I Learn Bushcraft?

There are many benefits to learning bushcraft. Learning bushcraft is a rewarding experience that equips you with the skills you need to navigate the challenging situations in the wild and helps you reconnect with your primal instincts and innate capabilities. Here is a list of reasons why you should consider learning bushcraft:

### You'll Learn Independence

Bushcraft teaches you the necessary skills to survive. By learning these skills, you will learn how to take care of yourself, fostering a sense of confidence and self-reliance in yourself. Learning basic life-saving skills such as building a fire, constructing a shelter, and getting clean water and food are wonderful forms of self-reliance that will teach you how to survive with minimal resources if you ever find yourself in an unfortunate situation.

### It Teaches You Critical Thinking and Problem-Solving Skills

Bushcraft skills help you develop the ability to analyze situations, find solutions, and adapt to new circumstances. You will need creative problem-solving skills and quick thinking to survive in the wilderness. These skills are also important for navigating other aspects of your life, including school projects and personal challenges.

### Creates Environmental Awareness

Bushcraft and outdoor skills deeply connect you to nature. As you learn to thrive in natural environments, you will become more environmentally conscious and appreciate the world around you. Using environmentally-friendly techniques will nurture a desire to save the planet.

### Makes You More Adaptable and Resourceful

As you know, you will have limited resources in the wild. Children who learn bushcraft skills become more self-reliant and resourceful as they navigate difficult situations using natural resources efficiently. They become more adaptable and believe they can find a way out in all situations, including those in their everyday lives.

### Makes You Physically Fit

Bushcraft skills require a lot of physical exertion, which is bound to make you physically stronger. These skills allow you to develop an appreciation for outdoor activities and become more physically active.

### You'll Gain Crisis Management Skills

You can save lives in emergencies with bushcraft skills. Crisis management skills such as emergency signaling, navigation, and learning first aid will prepare you for unexpected situations.

### Boosts Your Confidence and Resilience

Becoming self-reliant will boost your self-confidence. These essential life-saving skills make you believe you can overcome adversity and challenges. It makes you more resilient, and you begin to understand that you can handle life's uncertainties with composure and persistence.

### Opportunity to Educate Others

Once you become a pro at bushcraft, and if you're passionate about it, you can also teach these essential skills to others. Share your knowledge of these practical skills with your friends, family, and other kids in your school or the neighborhood.

### Outdoor Recreation

Bushcraft is an excellent way to enhance your amusement experiences. It will make your outdoor experiences, whether camping, backpacking, or hiking, significantly more enjoyable and adventurous.

You'll feel accomplished when you discover you can manage the fire safely, cook meals, and take on responsibilities involved in survival. These survival skills are useful because they make you self-reliant, humble, and nature-loving.

### Respect Nature and Leave No Trace Behind

Care for the environment and leave it how you found it. You can enjoy and benefit from nature without disturbing the ecosystem or leaving any traces of your presence. Here are some ways in which you can minimize your impact on the environment:

### Minimize Pollution

Be cautious of the waste you generate while in natural environments. Make sure to pack up all your litter and limit the use of disposable items. You must pick up after yourself and carefully dispose of your trash.

### Do Not Create New Trails

Use the established trails to prevent soil erosion and habitat disruption. Creating new trails can also cause damage to wildlife habitats and vegetation.

### Do Not Disturb the Wildlife

If you come across a wild animal, you may observe them from afar and try not to disturb or feed them. Feeding these wild animals can disrupt their diets and natural behaviors and may lead to unhealthy interactions between animals and humans.

### Use Sustainable Transportation

Make sure to use sustainable means of transportation to visit these natural areas. You may use your bike, carpool with your friends, or use public transportation to reduce your carbon footprint.

### Save Water

Take special care of your water usage while exploring nature. Being mindful of your water consumption can reduce the danger of water contamination through soap, detergents, or other pollutants.

### Educate Yourself

Learning about the wildlife and natural areas you visit will help you understand the fragility of your environment. It can lead you to make better decisions and utilize careful behaviors while you're out there.

### Do Not Disturb the Natural and Cultural Artifacts

Leave the natural or cultural artifacts as you found them. This includes plants, rocks, and historical relics. Avoid removing these artifacts and leave them for the next person to enjoy and appreciate.

### Inspire Others

You can share your knowledge and inspire others to care for the environment and the natural and cultural artifacts. You must encourage your loved ones to learn and obey the essential principles of the "Leave No Trace" movement.

You must respect nature by utilizing the techniques mentioned above to ensure that you leave minimal environmental impact. It is important to take care of the ecosystem's delicate balance to ensure that future generations also get to appreciate it. Everyone should play their part in protecting the environment.

### Bushcraft Activities Deepen Your Connection to the Natural World

Nature is the greatest teacher. Learning bushcraft skills allows you to connect and develop your relationship with nature. It has a healing effect that boosts happiness and physical and emotional well-being. It awakens your sense of peace. Here is how nature has a healing impact on humans:

### Enhances Your Observation and Awareness

Your awareness of your surroundings and observational skills are heightened with bushcraft. You will notice subtle environmental cues, such as recognizing edible vegetation, tracking wildlife, and identifying weather changes. Bushcraft will enhance your understanding of the world around you and your importance in it.

### Respect for Your Surroundings

Learning bushcraft helps you develop a deeper respect for nature. It empowers you to rely on natural resources to fulfill your needs and develop a sense of responsibility and gratitude for the environment that provides these resources.

### Mindfulness and Presence

Bushcraft exercises require one to remain present in the moment. It is important to practice mindfulness to stay safe and thrive in the wilderness.

### Connect to Traditional Knowledge

Many bushcraft skills are deep-rooted in the indigenous knowledge passed down through generations. You can strengthen your relationship with the natural world and connect with the wisdom of your ancestors by practicing these skills.

### Importance of Safety and Responsible Outdoor Behavior

You must be responsible during your outdoor adventures. Your actions impact yourself, others, and the environment. Here are some ways you can stay safe and enjoy the outdoors.

### Injury Prevention and Well-Being

You must adhere to the safety guidelines while learning bushcraft or other outdoor activities, including camping, hiking, and water sports. Behaving responsibly will help you stay secure while having fun. Keep yourself hydrated and wear appropriate clothing and gear to maintain good health.

### Environmental Conservation

You must protect the environment at all costs and refrain from littering, vandalism, and engaging in reckless behavior, as it can lead to uncontrolled fires and damage the ecosystems and natural habitats.

### Ethical Considerations

Respect people around you and engage in behavior that does not ruin anyone else's experience. Allow other people to connect with nature without any distractions. You must also be mindful of the cultural and historical sites and treat these sites with respect.

### Community and Social Responsibility

Prepare for emergencies and make sure you always adhere to the safety protocols. Moreover, try your best to follow the trail etiquette and avoid overcrowding a place.

# How to Plan the First Bushcraft Adventure

Do you want to know how to plan your first bushcraft adventure? You must prioritize comfort, safety, and enjoyment. Here are some tips to plan your bushcraft adventure:

### Choose a Safe Location

Choose a location that is safe, easily accessible, and has a manageable terrain.

### Check the Weather Forecast

Before setting out on an adventure, pack clothing and appropriate gear to deal with unexpected weather conditions. Prepare for rain as well.

### Appropriate Gear

You need a sleeping bag, a backpack, and clothing of your size that fits comfortably.

### Simple Shelter

Ensure you have a simple and steady shelter that is easy to assemble and protects you from other environmental elements.

### Food and Water

Plan your meals and snacks and ensure you have everything you need to make the food you need. Also, make sure you have access to clean water.

### Supervision

It is wise to be accompanied by a responsible and experienced adult.

### Basic Skills

Learn age-appropriate basic bushcraft skills such as identifying edible plants, setting up campfires, and using navigation tools like compasses.

### Fun Activities

Engage in fun activities like scavenger hunts, storytelling, watersports, stargazing, etc., to enhance your outdoor experience.

### Comfort Items

Pack your favorite blankie, toy, or pillow to feel better in the wild.

### First-Aid Kit

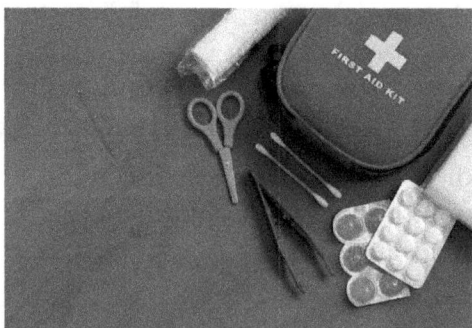

Ensure you have access to a first aid box to deal with injuries or illnesses.
*https://www.pexels.com/photo/first-aid-kit-on-gray-background-5673523/*

Ensure you have access to a first aid box to deal with injuries or illnesses.

In this section, you learned the basics of bushcraft. Remember that as you learn these essential survival skills, you must take care of yourself and remain prepared for emergencies. You can have the most fun while staying responsible and engaging in safe behaviors while taking care of the environment.

# Section 2: Bushcraft Gear

Taking a bushcraft kit with you on an outdoor adventure is essential for several reasons. First, it's a matter of survival and safety. A well-equipped bushcraft kit contains tools and gear crucial to keep you safe and secure in the wilderness. Whether cutting tools for various tasks, fire-starting equipment to provide warmth and cook food, or materials for building a shelter, these items are invaluable in challenging situations.

Furthermore, you become more self-sufficient outdoors, reducing your dependence on external assistance. This level of preparedness is necessary for emergencies, where your kit can mean the difference between comfort and difficulty. Beyond survival, a bushcraft kit allows you to maximize your use of natural resources. With the right tools and knowledge, you can adapt to your surroundings, finding shelter, fire, and sustenance solutions.

Likewise, you can cook hot meals, stay warm, and create a secure sleeping arrangement, which is vital for extended trips. It serves a dual purpose of providing safety and contains tools necessary for outdoor explorations.

In this chapter, you'll learn about bushcraft gear components, including the tools and equipment needed to make your outdoor adventures a breeze.

# Shelter and Sleep

Shelters are a makeshift outdoor home to make when you want to stay at a place for further exploration.

Shelters are a makeshift outdoor home to make when you want to stay at a place for further exploration. Sleeping sacks, tents, and tarps are some standard items used for shelter in the wild. They keep you cozy and dry in rainy weather and protect you from wandering bugs or insects that could harm you during sleep.

**Types of Shelters:** Although shelters come in different shapes and sizes, tents are the most feasible for a family adventure. These are portable homes set up for more than one person to use. Tarps are also popular as these waterproof blankets are compact to carry and can be set up instantly. You also have the option of a bivouac sack, which is a sleeping bag for your body. These snug sleeping sacks are also waterproof and insulated to keep you dry and warm. The type of shelter you pick will depend on the days you'll live outdoors, the number of people going, and the weather conditions.

**Setting up Your Shelter:** It's not difficult to set up a shelter as long as you know the proper steps to execute.

1. Find an even and clear spot if you're setting up a tent.
2. Lay out the tent and make a footprint for reference.

3. Assemble the tent poles and place them on the footprint you made earlier.

4. Attach the tent body to the pole structure, and it's all done.

While you won't find it hard to set up sleeping sacks or tarps, tents can come in several forms, and their assembly procedure can vary too. If you have trouble setting up the tent, review the instructions from the tent's user manual for better understanding. Just like you assembled the tent, you can disassemble it by reversing the order of instructions. When you've finished your trip, check the tent for damage, clean it, and store it properly so it can be used for your next outdoor adventure.

## Sleeping Essentials

Your bushcraft gear should contain sleeping essentials like sleeping bags, mats, and blankets to keep you extra comfy and protected from the weather.
https://www.pexels.com/photo/waterfall-seen-from-tent-15310519/

Besides packing shelter essentials, your bushcraft gear should contain sleeping essentials like sleeping bags, mats, and blankets to keep you extra comfy and protected from the weather. Although there are several sleeping essentials, it's best to pick travel-friendly quilts and blankets and even pack hammocks when exploring the wild in the summer.

## Cutting Tools

Knives are your trusty tools for cutting things during your camping adventures. They always come in handy, from making marshmallow sticks to opening canned packages. Likewise, camping axes and saws are excellent for chopping wood and making campfires. However, you must use these tools with extreme caution and under the supervision of a family member to ensure safety. After every outdoor trip, keep your cutting tools clean and sharp, and store them in perfect condition for the next trip.

**A bushcraft knife is easy to handle and use for many tasks.**
*Teejaybee, CC BY-NC-ND 2.0 DEED <https://creativecommons.org/licenses/by-nc-nd/2.0/>*
*https://www.flickr.com/photos/teejaybee/8591215307*

A bushcraft knife is not the regular household knife used to cut fruit in the kitchen; it's made of sturdy blade material and comes in many forms. You can purchase a bushcraft knife according to size preference and handle design. The right knife should fit comfortably in your hand, be durable, and suit your intended tasks, such as cutting, carving, or other outdoor needs.

### Fire-Making Gear

These tools are used mainly to create warm campfires, cook food, or even to signal for help if you need assistance during escapades. There are a variety of fire-starting tools and materials to pick from. Here are some common ones you can add to your bushcraft gear.

**Firesteel and Flint:** In old times, flint and steel were struck together to produce sparks and ignite dry tinder. Nowadays, modern firesteel comes with a steel rod to generate sparks, making fire-starting hassle-free. Firesteel is also much more reliable when used in extreme weather conditions.

**Firesteel and flint makes lighting a fire super easy.**

**Ferrocerium Rods:** Ferrocerium rods, often called ferro rods, create hot sparks when scraped with a hard object, like the back of a knife. They're highly durable and work in wet conditions, making them a dependable tool for igniting dry tinder in the wild.

**Waterproof Matches and Lighters:** Waterproof matches have treated heads that resist water and light even when damp, while lighters produce a flame when ignited. They are excellent backup tools for starting fires during camping or emergencies. However, you must keep lighters dry for reliable use.

**Tinder and Fuel:** Tinder and fuel are the unique ingredients for your campfire magic. They make the wood catch fire quickly, like adding sticks and paper to burn brightly.

### Containers and Hydration

**Water Containers:** Whether you want electrolyte water on the go or prefer drinking plain water, you'll need containers and water bottles. They ensure you stay hydrated by holding your water so you have enough to drink during outdoor adventures.

Water containers are important to keep you hydrated.
https://www.peakpx.com/526025/blue-and-stainless-steel-thermal-carafe

**Water Purification Tools:** You can add portable water purification gadgets to the bushcraft kit to ensure your drinking water is clean and safe. Water purification tablets, water filters for backpackers, and portable sediment filters can be used for water purification. You can pick a feasible method according to the adventure you are planning. Despite all these methods, you can still go for the old-school method of boiling water before drinking if you're not carrying any water purification gadget or tool.

### Navigation and Signaling

Navigation tools are your guides in the wilderness.
https://www.pexels.com/photo/person-holding-a-compass-3832684/

**Navigation Tools:** Navigation tools are your guides in the wilderness. They include maps and compasses that help you find your way when you're out exploring so you don't get lost.

**Signaling and Communication:** Signaling and communication tools are your way to send secret messages to your friends or call for help if you need it. They're like your adventure walkie-talkies and signal to get assistance when you're on exciting adventures.

### First Aid and Safety

**First Aid Kits:** First aid kits are your superhero kits for when you get a little hurt. They contain band-aids, medicine, and other things to help you feel better if you have a small injury during outdoor fun. This can include creams for insect bites.

**Safety Gear:** Safety gear is like your adventure superhero outfit. It includes headlamps to light your way, bear spray to keep animals away, and cool tools to keep you safe and make your outdoor experiences amazing.

Safety gear like a headlamp makes it easier for you to walk around the camp at night.
*https://www.wallpaperflare.com/man-standing-beside-camping-tent-wearing-headlamp-during-nighttime-man-using-headlamp-beside-cabin-tent-wallpaper-zmonu*

### Backpacks

**Choosing the Right Backpack:** Selecting the right backpack is like choosing the right-sized backpack for school. It's important because it should comfortably hold all your gear. Consider factors like size, capacity, and features based on the length and type of trip you are going on.

**Packing Your Backpack Efficiently:** Think of packing your backpack like organizing your school bag. Efficient packing involves placing heavier items closer to your back so that the load is well balanced, using compartments wisely, and keeping essential gear easily accessible. It ensures a comfortable and well-balanced load.

**Adjusting and Fitting Your Pack:** Adjusting and fitting your backpack is like wearing your school bag with the right straps and adjustments to keep it comfortable. Straps, hip belts, and shoulder straps should be adjusted to your body for a snug and well-distributed load, preventing discomfort during your outdoor journey.

Make sure you get the right backpack that's easy to carry and holds everything you need.
https://www.wallpaperflare.com/hiking-backpacks-on-grass-with-mountains-background-blue-and-red-camping-bag-on-green-grass-field-wallpaper-zhowh

## Clothing Essentials

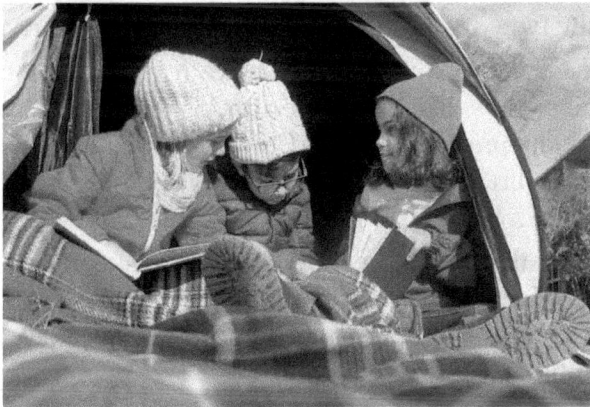

Dress right for the adventure when in the wild.
https://www.pexels.com/photo/children-in-winter-clothes-sitting-inside-a-tent-reading-books-6482318/

Dress right for the adventure when in the wild. You have three layers to consider:

**Base Layers:** These are cozy pajamas for the outdoors. These clothes are closest to your skin, designed to keep you warm and dry by wicking away sweat. They act like insulation in cold weather, trapping heat close to your body. Cotton is a wise choice.

**Mid-Layers:** Mid-layers are like your regular clothes for the outdoors. They provide insulation to keep you warm but are also breathable, preventing you from getting too sweaty. They are extra layers to stay cozy.

**Outer Layers:** Consider the outer layers your *superhero cape*. They shield you from the elements, like rain, wind, and snow. These layers keep you dry and protect you from the weather, ensuring you stay comfortable in harsh conditions.

**Headwear and Gloves:** Headwear and gloves are your secret armor, keeping you warm and protected against the cold. Hats keep your head warm, and gloves guard your hands. They're essential for comfort and prevent frostbite in chilly weather.

**Footwear**

**Hiking Boots vs. Trail Shoes:** Hiking boots are the heavy-duty, all-terrain vehicles of footwear. They provide strong ankle support and protection against rough trails and heavy loads. Trail shoes, however, are like sporty sneakers for the outdoors. They're lighter and more flexible, suitable for less demanding hikes and faster movement. Your choice depends on the type of terrain and the weight you'll be carrying.

**Socks and Gaiters:** Think of socks as your cozy cushioning for your feet, while gaiters are like leg protectors. Good-quality socks provide comfort and help prevent blisters. Conversely, gaiters shield your legs and boots from dirt, rocks, and moisture, especially in rugged or wet conditions.

**Foot Care in the Wilderness:** Foot care is like looking after your favorite shoes. Maintain healthy feet by managing blisters, keeping your feet dry, and choosing proper footwear for an enjoyable and pain-free outdoor adventure.

# Ten Essential Items for Bushcraft Gear

These items are crucial for safety and survival in the outdoors. Each item serves a specific purpose to prepare you for various situations. Here are the ten essentials and their importance.

### 1. Navigation

**Map:** A detailed, up-to-date topographic map of the area you'll be exploring.

**Compass:** A reliable compass for navigation, especially in areas without clear trails or signage.

You need a map and a compass to navigate.
https://www.pexels.com/photo/compass-placed-on-a-world-map-8828681/

### 2. Insulation

**Extra Clothing:** Layers to help you stay warm and dry, including a hat and gloves.

### 3. Illumination

**Headlamp/Flashlight:** Provides light in low-light conditions or emergencies.

### 4. First Aid Supplies

**First Aid Kit:** Treats injuries and medical emergencies in the field.

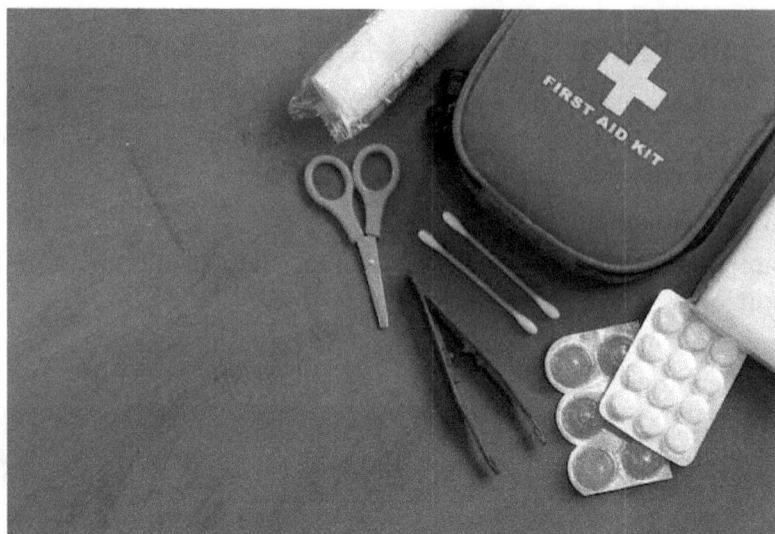

**A first aid kit will help with emergency situations.**

### 5. Fire Starter

**Firesteel, Waterproof Matches, or Lighter**: Critical for starting fires in emergencies, for warmth, cooking, and signaling.

### 6. Repair Tools and Kits

**Multi-Tool and Repair Kits**: Useful for gear repair and other tasks that may arise during your trip.

### 7. Nutrition

**Extra Food:** Non-perishable, high-energy snacks that can sustain you if your trip takes longer than expected.

### 8. Hydration

**Water and Filtration/Purification:** You need access to clean drinking water and avoid waterborne illnesses by using water purification methods.

### 9. Emergency Shelter

**Emergency Blanket or Tarp:** Provides shelter and protection from the elements in unexpected situations.

A tarp is useful if it starts raining or if you need to rest.

### 10. Sun Protection

**Sunscreen, Sunglasses, and a Hat:** Protect yourself from sunburn and UV exposure, especially in high-altitude or snow-covered environments.

The ten essentials are designed to help you navigate, survive, and stay safe in the wilderness. Remember to customize your gear based on your outdoor adventure's specific conditions and location.

# Optional Gear for Comfort and Convenience

If your trip is short and you won't be doing much exploration, consider these items for comfort:

- Camp Chair
- Multi-Tool
- Solar Charger
- Insect Repellent
- Camp Pillow
- Cookware Set
- Camp Stove
- Portable Water Heater
- Camp Shower
- Portable Coffee Maker

# Bushcraft Gear for Specific Seasons

As explained earlier, you must consider several factors when preparing your gear. Besides your personal requirements, the biggest influential factors are the weather and terrain. Here are some bushcraft gear samples for different seasons – so you know which items to pack. Please remember that the essential items listed above are already included in the gear but not mentioned here.

### Gear List for Woodlands (Spring/Summer)

- Additional clothing that is lightweight and has breathable layers
- Bug repellent
- Folding saw or small hatchet (for wood processing)
- Insect head net

### Gear List for Deserts (Fall/Winter)

- Sun-protective clothing and layers for cold nights
- Wide-brimmed hat
- Extra sunscreen and lip balm
- Bandana or shemagh (for protecting your face from sun and dust)

### Gear List for Mountains (Winter)

**Know the specific challenges and conditions of the environment and season you'll be venturing into.**

*https://www.pexels.com/photo/snow-on-rocky-mountain-peak-19168467/*

- Insulated and waterproof layers
- Crampons and ice ax (for snowy or icy conditions)
- Snow goggles
- Avalanche safety gear (if in avalanche-prone areas)
- Snowshoes (for deep snow)

Know the specific challenges and conditions of the environment and season you'll be venturing into. Customize your gear list accordingly and ensure you have the skills and knowledge to use each item effectively in those conditions. Additionally, always inform someone about your trip plans and expected return time when heading to more remote or challenging environments.

# Section 3: Cordage and Knots

Think about building a shelter in the woods. You will use many materials like branches and leaves. Now, imagine that you need to catch some fish. You may need a net. If you do not have a backpack, tie up your belongings to carry them easier. While ducking and dodging trees or shrubs, some of your clothing can get ripped, which you will need to repair, especially if you are spending extended periods in the wild. From your shelter to your tools and your traps for animals, cordage is useful for many of your bushcraft needs. Therefore, you must be skilled in using and tying knots in ways that can help with a broad range of issues that come up in nature.

**Cordage is a fancy word for rope or string.**

Cordage is a fancy word for rope or string. Naming all the uses for cordage in the wild is almost impossible because, with rope, only your imagination limits you. However, it helps to know a few basics when you are starting. Carrying a role of cordage in your pocket can come in handy in multiple situations you would not normally think of. Take a look around your house and see all the places where cord, string, and ropes are used. No survival kit is complete with it. So, what happens if you forget to take rope on a trip into the bush? True survivalists use their surroundings to their advantage. Cordage in the wild is abundant, with both plant and animal sources. Nature gives you everything you need. This section will teach you how to use cordage in different ways and how to identify cordage materials in the wilderness.

## Cordage and Its Many Forms

Cordage can take many forms, including natural and synthetic materials. Your cordage can either be neatly packed rope or line you brought on the trip with you or something you crafted from other items you had on you, depending on how innovative and creative you are. Historically, cordage was one of the first significant technological leaps of Stone Age people. The invention of cordage in different forms helped hunter-gatherers travel more easily, hunt with more efficiency, and, later on, construct systems for watering crops and constructing boats for sailing. The use of cordage is only limited by your expertise and your imagination. Therefore, understanding the basics of cordage use could transform the way you think about survival as you constantly discover new ways to use it.

## Natural Sources of Cordage Material

The purpose of bushcraft is to know how to survive in the wilderness with limited access to resources. Whether you are forcefully flung into a survival situation or lose your rope on a camping trip, knowing how to make cordage from natural material is a specialized skill that can be life-saving. To the trained eye and skilled hands, nature is a general store. For plant or animal materials to be suitable for cordage, they must meet a few conditions; namely, they must be strong, flexible, and easy to tie. Not every organism in the woods meets this criteria, and the geographical area you are in also has its unique conditions that will affect the cordage you can harness. Therefore, you need a background understanding of a few basic principles. Mastering the bush is all about knowing what to look for and how to craft it into exactly what you need.

### Plant Fibers

Many plants can be used for cordage as long as their fibers are strong and flexible. First, you must be sure that a plant or a tree is not toxic when you handle it. This is why any survivalist must educate themselves about the different species of plants in the areas they explore. One of the easiest ways to get cordage from plants is to find a tree with some dry bark that you can easily strip. Underneath the bark, you will find a fibrous cambium layer, the soft, stringy material on the surface of the tree, and the back of the bark. You notice the fibrous cambium makes strings when you rip the dry bark off. You also have the option of stripping wet bark and allowing it to dry in the sun. Be mindful that you can damage trees and kill them, so make sure not to cut too deeply into the trunk. Some leaves are also suitable for cordage. The key is to find long, stringy materials that you can manipulate, bend, and tie.

### Animal Sinew

Unlike plant cordage, which can pretty much be used immediately, animal sinew requires some processing. Traditional culture used big game like elk or deer from which to extract sinew. The long tendons in the legs of these giant beasts are the best part to use for cordage.

You will first need to cut the tendons carefully from the legs with a sharp knife. It is best if someone skilled and knowledgeable helps you with this.

Next, you must clean off all the excess meat and fat. Once the sinew is cleaned, you will need to dry it for a few days. Once all the moisture is out of the sinew, pound it with a hammer until it smooths out. This beating increases the strength and flexibility of the sinew. Lastly, you must twist the strands of sinew together and stretch them out to be useful for wilderness applications.

# Commercial Cordage Options

Most of the time, you will not be in the bush due to an unfortunate accident or survival event. Therefore, you will be able to carry the cordage of your choice on you. When choosing which types of string or ropes to use, you must consider how adaptable they are in various situations, how heavy they are because you will be carrying them, and how strong and flexible the cord is. The most commonly preferred cordage options for bushcraft are nylon and paracord. Scientists are always developing strong and lightweight materials, so there are always new varieties of outdoor cordage to try at specialized camping stores. Each of these materials has its benefits and disadvantages, so you must figure out what works best for your goals.

## Paracord

Paracord is a type of kernmantle rope, meaning it has an interior wrapped in woven fabrics.
*David J. Fred, CC BY-SA 2.5 <https://creativecommons.org/licenses/by-sa/2.5>, via Wikimedia Commons: https://commons.wikimedia.org/wiki/File:Paracord-Commercial-Type-III.jpg*

Paracord is a type of kernmantle rope, meaning it has an interior wrapped in woven fabrics. Much like nylon, paracord is strong and holds its shape quite well over time. One of the advantages of paracord is that it does not hold moisture like nylon, so it will not develop mold or mildew in moist environments. Paracord is relatively cheap compared to other rope materials with a similar strength. The downside of using paracord rope is that it can become tangled, which is an issue for someone with limited space in a backpack in the wilderness and who is constantly traveling. Furthermore, paracord tends to come in long sections, which could make it even more difficult to store.

## Nylon

Nylon rope is the strongest synthetic rope on the market.

Nylon rope is the strongest synthetic rope on the market, and its flexibility makes the rope shock absorbent, meaning that if something was attached to the rope and it fell, it reduces the chances of getting damaged. Nylon returns to its original size after it has been stretched and does not break easily. Plus, its durability and flexibility allow it to be used in many sticky situations that you can run into outdoors. The cons of using nylon rope are that it absorbs a lot of water, which weakens the rope and shrinks the material when wet, so it is probably not great for moist environments like forests.

# Fundamental Knots

Having some knowledge of knots you can quickly remember will make you a shining star in the bush. You'd be surprised how often you find yourself having to tie objects together in the wilderness. Your effectiveness in the woods is greatly increased when you know how to use your cordage properly. Freestyling knots can be dangerously ineffective and have disastrous outcomes. Therefore, you must be educated on how to use your rope, string, and any other cordage well.

## Square Knot

The square knot is used to tie a rope to an object. In a wilderness scenario, a square knot can tie bundles together, making objects like branches easier to carry. In some cases, square knots are tied around open wounds to stop bleeding. Therefore, this amazing knot can be used in numerous ways.

1. To tie a square knot, begin by passing one end of a rope or string over another.

2. Then, take the same end and pass it underneath the other end of the rope.

3. Repeat the crossing motion you did with the two remaining sections of rope.

4. Pull on both ends to tighten the knot. You can repeat the process, making a few knots on top of one another for more security.

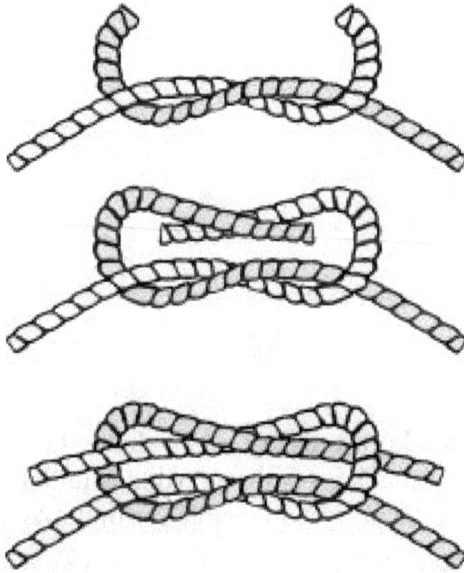

The square knot is used to tie a rope to an object.

This is one of the most basic knots to tie, and many people learned it when they began tying their shoelaces.

### Bowline

The bowline knot is used to secure a rope to a standing object like a tree or a pole. In the bush, this knot can tie down a shelter or belongings you do not want to lose.

1. For the first step of tying a bowline, you must create a loop in your cordage.

2. Next, grab the rope's end and pass it underneath the loop before pulling it through the center of the hole you have created.

3. Now, wrap the end of the rope you have passed through the loop around the standing section of the cordage.

4. Then push the rope back through the loop you created and then pull to tighten.

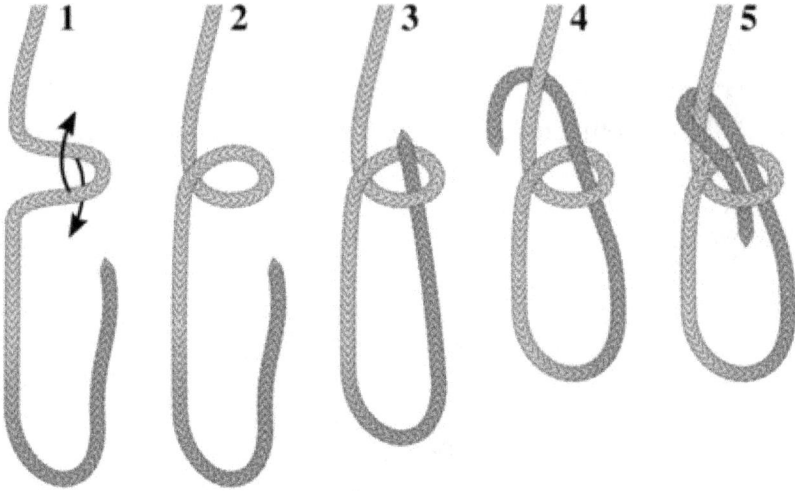

The bowline knot is used to secure a rope to a standing object like a tree or a pole.
*Buz11, CC BY-SA 4.0 <https://creativecommons.org/licenses/by-sa/4.0>, via Wikimedia Commons: https://commons.wikimedia.org/wiki/File:Bowline_tying.png*

## Taut-Line Hitch

The taut-line hitch knot is a very useful sliding knot to secure or carry items. The beauty of this knot is that it tightens under a load and can be slid easily for release, making it adaptable for multiple applications.

1. Start by looping a rope around the item, like a bucket handle or a post.

2. Take the rope's end and make another loop around the standing line. The loop should be made working towards the post your rope is around.

3. Now, make another loop around the standing line outside of the loop you had previously made.

4. After tightening the knot, you will be able to make the loop on the end of the rope bigger or smaller by sliding the knot back and forth.

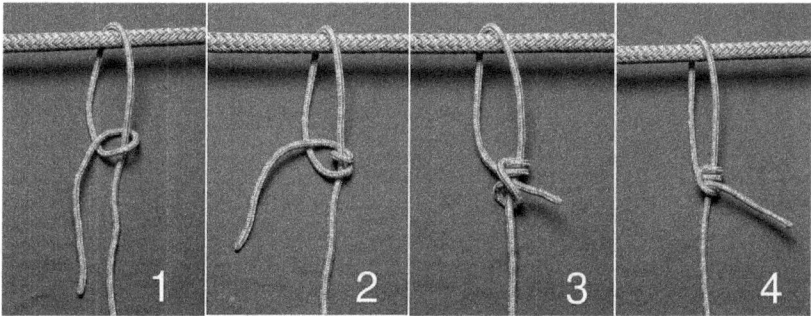

**The taut-line hitch knot is a very useful sliding knot to secure or carry items.**

## Clove Hitch

Clove hitch knots are used to secure a rope to a horizontal pole, stick, or branch. This knot is great for suspending valuables like pots or food out of the reach of various animals in the woods. The knot has also been used for rock climbing and sailing. However, note that a clove hitch knot can come loose when faced with enough tension, so it is best used in combination with other knots.

- Wrap your cordage around a horizontal pole or stick to tie a clove hitch.

- Next, cross the end of your rope over the already-wrapped section around the stick.

- Then thread the rope's end under the second loop you made and pull to tighten.

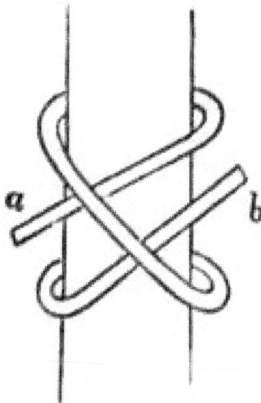

**Clove hitch knots are used to secure a rope to a horizontal pole, stick, or branch.**

# Choosing the Right Knot

The knot you choose will depend on what you are trying to achieve by tying your rope of string. Consider asking whether you need a string knot that can support a lot of weight or an adjustable knot. Other questions you can ask yourself include: will a simple knot be sufficient, or do you need a knot that can be easily loosened? By analyzing your goals and then exploring the knots you have learned, you can match the exact knot you need with the task you want to complete.

## Tips, Tricks, and Common Mistakes

Some common mistakes when using cordage are not double-checking your knots and using the wrong kind of rope. Different rope types are unsuited for certain conditions, and some knots are incompatible with some materials. So, ensure you use the right material paired with the right knots while carefully double or even triple-checking your knots to prevent accidents. The biggest tip that can be given regarding cordage is to make sure that it is both durable and flexible so that it can be used for multiple wilderness applications. Ask at a camping supply shop as often their staff are quite knowledgeable on which ropes to use.

# Section 4: Bushcraft Shelters

Your most basic needs are food, air, water, clothing, and shelter. If you are ever in a survival situation in the wilderness, shelter is one of the first needs to be taken care of. Constructing an effective shelter should be at the top of your priority list. In some circumstances, you may feel that lighting a fire should be your first priority. However, in some emergencies, you should build a shelter first. Most people take a tent when they go out into nature for recreation. However, to be a skillful survivalist, you cannot rely on store-bought shelters because you never know when you will not have access to one.

**You have to have proper shelter when you're outdoors.**
*https://www.pickpik.com/tent-shelter-homeless-hut-cover-tarp-rectangular-117012*

Different environments need different shelters. To be adaptable in all situations, you have to be aware of multiple construction techniques and the many kinds of structure options you have. Each ecosystem has a unique personality that responds to the actions you take. You cannot do the same thing in the rainforest as you would in the snow of Siberia. Using what is available is the key to survival. Therefore, you must learn how to look at the world around you as a "natural" hardware store you can use to find raw materials. By adjusting how you think about nature, you will find that everything you need is right at your fingertips.

## Why Shelter Is Important

There are many reasons why shelter is typically the first thing on the list to sort out for survival. Firstly, you need protection from the elements, sun, rain, and wind. Secondly, especially at night, you must find a way to maintain your body temperature. The normal body temperature for a person is 98.6 F. If your temperature drops below 95 F, you are experiencing hypothermia, which means your body temperature is too low and you are in danger. So, keeping yourself warm is closely tied to keeping yourself alive.

An elevated shelter, especially in the jungle, can protect you from snakes and insects on the ground. Therefore, a shelter is not just for your warmth but is also extremely important for your safety. Furthermore, having a certain level of comfort allows you to sleep better. A lack of sleep messes with your mind, so you will not be as sharp, and your responses will be much slower. In the wilderness, you need mental clarity to make good decisions that will enhance your probability of survival.

A shelter can also help you hide from predators. Building a discreet shelter that blends in with its background could help you avoid drawing attention from any animals that could harm you. Although camouflaging your shelter will not keep you 100 percent safe, it gives you an edge that could swing the odds of escaping an attack in your favor. If you are in a dangerous area where predators are roaming, your best bet is to stay hidden.

Your campsite is the hub of your survival that you will return to regularly to eat and sleep. Your shelter is the wilderness home that you will use as a place to keep a fire going to cook and boil water, as well as a place where you can store much-needed survival materials. You need a place to regroup and return to so you can keep your sanity in the wild. Your shelter gives you peace of mind so you can remain calm and operate at your highest level. Therefore, when you are in the bush, you should work from building a shelter and then cater to your other needs. Shelter construction is a high-energy activity, so you probably want to get it out of the way as soon as possible.

# Key Principles of Shelter Construction

You may be looking at your cleverly built shelter made from natural materials and giving yourself a pat on the back for a job well done, but there are some boxes you must tick before you attempt to use your shelter. A leaking, cold shelter may be better than nothing. Still, you can exponentially increase your comfort and safety by ensuring your shelter is wind-resistant, waterproof, and insulated to keep you warm. Additionally, you also want to take measures to keep as many bugs and spiders away as possible.

### Insulation

Insulation means keeping warmth in while it's cold outside. Even in more temperate regions, temperatures can quickly drop at night. Cold weather can be a death sentence, so insulation must be taken seriously. Bark, leaves, wood chips, and plants can be layered strategically to keep the cold out. Do not sleep directly on the ground; this is a quick way to lose heat. Use a wood floor made with branches, and layer leaves and branches at the bottom and top to keep you elevated off the ground. Your insulation material should cover any gaps in the structure so the heat from your breath and body can be kept in the shelter while the cold air from outside is kept out. Use what you have available, so blankets, sleeping bags, cushions, clothing, and even newspapers can be used to insulate yourself.

### Waterproofing

Not many things on the planet are as bad as cold and wet moisture preventing you from sleeping. Whether it is dew in the early morning or the pouring rain in a forest, making your shelter waterproof will keep you warm and comfortable. Waterproofing follows a similar blueprint to insulation because they both use similar materials. Strategically positioning your camp where water doesn't gather is the first step to waterproofing your shelter. Next, you want materials you can layer and weave together so the gaps in your shelter's wooden frame can be closed.

Moss and pine needles are great for waterproofing, especially in cold places where it often snows. You can also use grass, reeds, and leaves to keep all water out. Sometimes, everything does not go as planned, so keep some extra material nearby to patch your shelter as needed and carry a tarp in your kit.

Having a waterproof tent will keep the rain at bay and you can have a restful sleep.
*GabeD, CC BY-NC-ND 2.0 DEED< https://creativecommons.org/licenses/by-nc-nd/2.0/>*
*https://www.flickr.com/photos/augustuspics/7043841387*

## Wind Protection

Wind protection works hand in hand with insulation and waterproofing. Again, the materials you choose to shelter yourself from wind must fill all the openings in your shelter. A tip for wind protection is keeping the entryway to your shelter small because less air will be able to get in. Another useful trick to remember is to use cords to tie down your insulation material so the wind does not blow it away. Everything in your shelter must be solid so that the weather does not destroy the structure. Use your surroundings to your advantage and build close to a rock formation or in between trees so that your habitat can help you block the strong wind.

## Natural Shelters

Sometimes, it is easier to find a shelter than it is to build one. You are trying to work smart – not hard – in the bush. Using what's already available is the key that everyone with survival knowledge must fully understand. Look around and see what you can use to your advantage. Be creative and think outside of the box. When you find natural shelters, you must be vigilant because they may already be an animal or insect owner of that shelter. Your senses should always be on high alert because nature can be unforgiving. Being in the wild is fun, but your safety should always be your first concern. Look for a dry place that shields you from wind and where you can make a fire to keep predators away. Make sure to clean the structure before you use it because there may be unwanted creepy crawlies looking to enter through cracks and holes.

**You can find shelter in nature to keep you safe.**

Below is a list of natural shelters you can use to save time and energy. Be on the lookout for the following naturally occurring structures:
- Caves
- Rock formations
- Hollow trees
- Fallen trees
- Thick bushes or shrubs
- Cliffs
- Evergreen trees
- Low land formations
- Overhangs

# Building a Shelter

Now that you understand the principles and importance of building a shelter, you need some practical tips and ideas for how you can go about constructing the best shelter in any situation. Wilderness shelters are easy to build, low-effort, and use materials that are readily available around you. You do not need anything fancy; it just needs to be functional. Remember, when you spend time in nature, you should leave things the way you found them, so always clean up your campsite before you leave to respect the plants and animals that receive you as their guest.

### Lean-to Shelter

A lean-to structure is simple to build and can be put up in various places.
https://commons.wikimedia.org/wiki/File:Field-expedient_lean-to_and_fire_reflector.jpg

A lean-to structure is simple to build and can be used in various places.

- First, you need to find either a rock face or two strong trees that are close together.
- If you are using a rock face, find straight branches about the same size and lean them against the hard surface.
- Next, tie smaller sticks horizontally across the sticks you have leaned vertically against the rock face.
- Lastly, fill in the gaps with insulation like leaves or moss.
- If you are using two trees, there is one extra step. You must secure a long branch horizontally between two trees. You can repeat the same steps as you would for a rock face by angling sticks from the ground against the stick you secure at about your waist height.
- You will then fill the gaps with leaves and greenery to provide insulation.
- Don't forget to insulate the ground as well.

**A-Frame Shelter**

This shelter is a little more complicated than the lean-to, but it has the added advantage of camouflaging the shelter well and having a bit more insulation for colder environments.

- Find a thick, strong branch to use as a ridge pole. Lean this branch against a strong tree and tie it down with some cord.
- Next, collect more branches that you will lean on the center pole you created with the first branch. Ensure the sticks are angled to firmly stabilize and tie them down on the ground.
- Collect debris like leaves, pine branches, or moss to insulate your shelter. Crawl into the shelter and pack additional debris in the doorway to seal you up inside snugly and comfortably.

## Tarp Shelters

**A tarp shelter is one of the easiest structures to build.**
*Jomegat, CC BY-SA 3.0 <https://creativecommons.org/licenses/by-sa/3.0>, via Wikimedia Commons: https://commons.wikimedia.org/wiki/File:Pole_tarp_and_rope_shelter_4855.JPG*

A tarp shelter is one of the easiest structures to build. Carrying a tarp with you in the wilderness can be useful for shelter and collecting water. Tarps are more waterproof and warmer than shelters, using debris like sticks and leaves for insulation. Therefore, a tarp is an amazing survival tool.

- Start by laying your tarp flat on the ground and securing the corners with heavy rocks.
- Find a strong stick and place it upright in the middle of your tarp. You can dig a hole for the stick to secure it better.
- Lastly, insulate your floor with wood and branches to keep your body from absorbing the cold from the ground.

### Emergency Shelter with Limited Resources

You will not always find everything you need for your shelter, so you must use what you have on hand. All of the shelters described above can be created with limited resources. Feel free to get creative. You can use the materials you have on you for a shelter. Pollution sometimes provides useful materials like plastic or paper that can be used as frames or insulation in a shelter. A tarp or a raincoat can also be repurposed as waterproofing. The wilderness and emergency survival situations demand that you use anything you have on hand to your benefit. You just have to look at your resources with an engineer's eyes.

## Choosing the Best Campsite

Choosing a great campsite to build a structure is half of the job. A few considerations must be kept in mind when finding the perfect spot. Firstly, ensure that you are at least 200 hundred meters away from any water source to prevent flooding. Check the drainage of the campsite to ensure that water flows away well and does not gather in that spot. Try to find a solid surface like gravel or hard ground. You want a campsite with minimal pests and away from any animal homes. Look around to make sure that there are no rocks or trees that can fall on you. The best campsite is where it is dry with some protection from the wind. If you are in an area where it is extremely hot, finding a shady spot could also be helpful.

# Section 5: Firecraft

Having the skill to build a fire is something everyone should learn. It's not just helpful for starting a campfire. It can be used in so many different ways. Imagine you're out in the wild, and the night is getting dark and scary. That's when a fire can be your best friend.

It's like a warm hug from Mother Nature, keeping you toasty when it's chilly outside.
*https://www.pexels.com/photo/people-sitting-in-front-of-bonfire-in-desert-during-nighttime-1703314/*

First of all, a fire can keep you safe and cozy. It's like a warm hug from Mother Nature, keeping you toasty when it's chilly outside. Plus, the crackling flames can scare away any curious wild animals considering visiting your campsite.

But that's not all. A fire can also be a secret message to your friends or rescuers in the dark. If you need help, a blazing fire sends a beacon saying, "I'm here, come find me!" So, in some situations, a fire can literally save your life.

However, building a fire is more challenging than it may seem. It needs three things to work: air, heat, and fuel. However, here's the tricky part. It's super hard to get all those things to cooperate on a rainy day, and if you're tired and a bit scared, it becomes even tougher.

Imagine using a whole bunch of matches and still being unable to start a fire. What would you do then? That's the adventure of fire-making. Sometimes it's easy, and sometimes it's a real challenge, but once you master it, you'll feel like a wilderness expert!

# Preparing the Fire Area

Preparing your fire area is important to ensure a successful and safe campfire.

### 1. Choosing the Right Spot

First, you should pick a location that's already safe for making a fire. Look for places like the top of a big rock or a sandy area. It's best to find a spot that's sheltered from the wind. If you can, find a big boulder or rock behind which you can place your fire area. This way, more of the fire's heat will bounce back to keep you warm.

### 2. Clear the Way

To be smart and safe, clear a circle at least 10 feet wide for your fire area. That means removing anything that can catch fire easily, like leaves, grass, and pine needles. This will prevent the fire from spreading where you don't want it to. Dig a shallow hole in the ground to create a fire pit if you can. This makes your fire safer and makes it easier to light when there's a breeze. If digging a pit isn't an option, you can make a ring of rocks around your fire area. These rocks will help contain the flames and stay warm even after the fire dies.

### 3. Snowy Situations

If you're in a snowy area, you can't just plop a fire on top of the snow. You'll need to create a sturdy foundation for your fire. Gather logs or large sticks to make a deck. This way, your fire won't melt into the snow.

**You need to have a good foundation to start a fire in the snow.**

# Materials for Your Fire

Once your spot is set up, it's time to collect the materials you need for your fire. To keep a fire going strong all night, you'll need more wood than you might think. You'll need three main types of wood: tinder, kindling, and logs.

- **Tinder:** This is the stuff you light first to start the fire. It needs to be super dry and easy to catch fire. The dryer your tinder, the better it works. You can use things like dry leaves, paper, or even special fire-starting materials you might have.

- **Kindling:** These are thin sticks and small branches that you feed the fire to help it grow. They're like the appetizer for your fire, getting it ready for the big logs. Make sure your kindling is dry, too.

- **Logs:** The main event! These bigger pieces of wood keep your fire burning steadily. They provide the lasting warmth and light you need during your camping adventure.

# Tinder Types

When building a fire, having the right tinder can make your life much easier. Think of tinder as the magical stuff that catches fire first and helps you get that cozy campfire going. Below, explore different types of tinder you can use:

### 1. Carry Your Tinder

If you're well-prepared and have a survival kit, you can save time and effort by taking some tinder with you. Good tinder materials to pack include fine steel wool, shredded paper, waxed paper, or small pieces of fatwood (which comes from a resinous tree). You can even check your pockets for dryer lint; it's usually dry and makes excellent tinder.

### 2. Nature's Tinder

If you didn't bring your own tinder, and it's a wet day, don't worry. Mother Nature has you covered. Look for dry pine needles, grass, or dried rabbit or deer droppings. These can work as natural tinder. You can also find small pieces of dry wood or bark. And if the ground isn't helping, you can turn to punk. Punk is rotted wood inside trees that have been dead for a while. Birch or cedar tree bark can be shredded and used as tinder. Birch trees have white, papery bark, and cedar trees look like redwood or pine trees but have flat leaves. Break them up or shred them to create a loose bundle.

### Hunting for Firewood

Now, it's time to find the bigger pieces for your fire. Search for firewood in places protected from the weather, like under a big tree or beneath a piece of bark. Once you've got your fire going, you can put damp wood near the fire to dry it out for later use.

# Building Your Fire

There are many ways to build a fire, but they all start by lighting small bits of dry tinder. Arrange the tinder so the flames are shielded from the wind but can still get some oxygen. You can make a teepee shape with your tinder and small sticks or lean a bundle of tinder against a log. When you see flames in your tinder, gently blow on the fire to add oxygen and carefully feed it with small kindling sticks. Add one or two sticks at a time until your fire burns nicely. Once you have a strong fire, you can add larger sticks and, eventually, logs.

# Fire Starters and Fire-Starting Materials

Once you've got your tinder ready, the next step is to ignite it, and you need reliable tools to do that. Some survival books discuss starting fires with flint, fire plows, or bow drills. These methods can be fun to learn but are not very practical when you're cold, scared, wet, and alone in the woods. You need quick, easy, and foolproof ways to start a fire.

## 1. Store-Bought Fire Starters

You can find some fantastic fire-starting products in camping stores. Here are a couple of them:

- **Waterproof Matches:** These matches are lifesavers, as they light easily, even in wet conditions. Just make sure to keep the striker paper dry by packing them in a sealed container.

- **Disposable Lighters:** These are cheap and usually work even if they get wet. You can dry it out if yours gets wet, and it should work fine. Carrying both waterproof matches and a lighter whenever you go hiking is a good idea.

## 2. Using the Sun's Power

On sunny days, you can use sunlight to start a fire.
https://www.pexels.com/photo/abstract-beach-bright-clouds-301599/

On sunny days, you can use sunlight to start a fire. A small magnifying glass or even a pair of eyeglasses can do the trick. In fact, anything that reflects sunlight can help create a fire. People have even ignited fires using glass bowls on wood decks, crystals in windows, or drinking glasses left on windowsills. You are harnessing the power of the sun!

### 3. DIY Fire-Starting Materials

If you don't have store-bought fire starters, don't worry. You can make your own with simple things you may have:

- **Tortilla Chips:** Hold a flame from a match or lighter under a tortilla chip for a few seconds, and it will catch fire. Light-colored chips with less seasoning work best.
- **Toilet Paper and Candle Wax**: Coat individual toilet paper squares with melted candle wax. These catch fire quickly and burn steadily.
- **Cotton Balls and Petroleum Jelly**: Dip cotton balls in petroleum jelly (like Vaseline). They catch fire immediately and burn strongly for quite a while.
- **Fire Paste:** Sold in tubes, you squeeze it onto wood and light it. It ignites instantly.
- **Fuel Tablets:** Various solid fuel tablets that burn well and provide enough heat to cook over are available.
- **Magnesium Block Scrapings**: You can buy blocks of magnesium with a flint edge. Shave some magnesium flakes onto your tinder, then strike the flint with a knife to create sparks that set the magnesium flakes on fire. It works even when damp.

### 4. Improvise with What You Have

If you didn't bring fire-starting materials, think about what you did bring that could be used as a substitute. Do you have lint in your pocket, tissues, a candy bar wrapper, or a piece of paper you can tear off and shred?

# Basic Fire-Starting Methods

- **Tinder Bundle:** Gather dry leaves, grass, and small sticks. Make a little bundle out of them. Now, use matches or a lighter to set the bundle on fire. Blow on it gently to make the flames grow.
- **Fire Starter Kit:** Get a special kit with waterproof matches, cotton balls, and a striker. Learn how to light the matches and use the cotton balls as fire starters.
- **Magnifying Glass:** Use a magnifying glass to catch the sun's rays on sunny days. Aim the glass at a pile of dry stuff like leaves or paper and watch it start to smoke and catch fire. Magic!

You can use a magnifying glass to start a fire.
*Dave Gough, CC BY 2.0 DEED <https://creativecommons.org/licenses/by/2.0/>*
*https://www.flickr.com/photos/spacepleb/1505372433*

- **Candle and Tinder:** Light a candle with a grown-up's help and use the candle's flame to start a fire in a safe and controlled way. This helps you learn without touching big flames.

# Intermediate Fire-Building Techniques

- **Teepee Fire Lay:** Arrange small sticks in a teepee shape around your tinder bundle. This lets the air get in and makes your fire grow. Add bigger sticks as your fire gets bigger.

Arrange small sticks in a teepee shape around your tinder bundle.
*https://www.pickpik.com/fire-camping-camp-nature-campfire-forest-91264*

- **Log Cabin Fire Lay:** Make a little log cabin out of your sticks with your tinder bundle inside. Light the bundle, and the log cabin falls apart as it burns, adding more sticks to the fire.

Make a little log cabin out of your sticks with your tinder bundle inside.
https://pixabay.com/vectors/campfire-wood-fire-firewood-31930/

- **Lean-To Fire Lay:** Build a little shelter with sticks, leaving one side open like a tent. Put your tinder inside, light it up, and the fire will catch on. This is good for windy days.

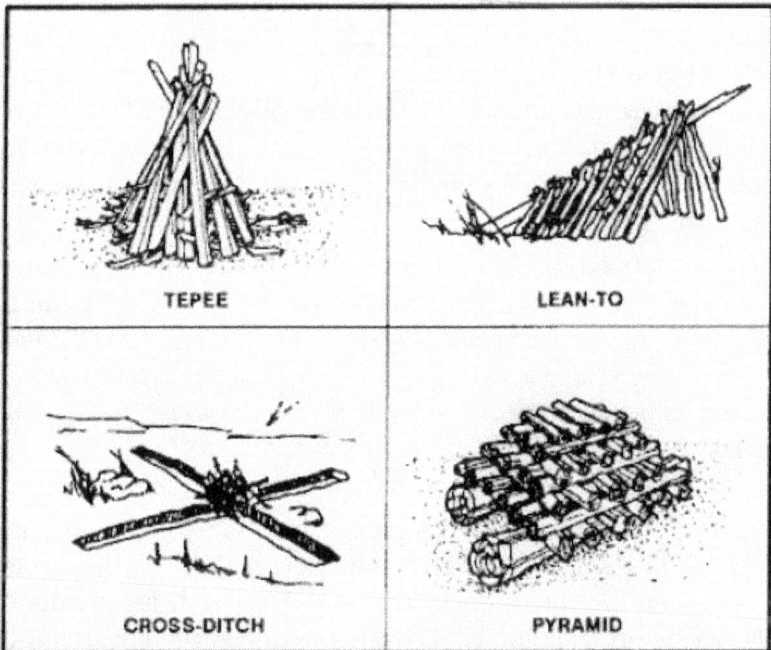

Build a little shelter with sticks, leaving one side open like a tent.
https://commons.wikimedia.org/wiki/File:Methods_of_laying_fires.jpg

# Advanced Fire-Starting Methods (with Grown-Up Help)

- **Fire Starter Tools**: These tools make hot sparks when you scrape them. A grown-up can help you use them to light your tinder.

- **Flint and Steel**: Strike a piece of special rock (like flint) against a steel striker to make sparks. Use the sparks to light your tinder.

- **Bow Drill**: The bow drill is like magic. It needs a spindle, a hearth board, a bow, and a socket. By moving the bow fast, you can heat and light the tinder. It takes practice!

- **Fire by Friction**: These methods involve rubbing things together to create heat, like the hand drill or fire plow. They're tricky and need a lot of practice. Grown-ups can help you learn.

**Disclaimer:** Always have an adult present before starting a fire.

# Staying Warm and Staying Safe

To keep warm at night, you can heat rocks next to the fire and place them under your clothes or in your shelter. Be careful because they'll be hot! Don't put rocks that have been sitting in water or that have small pockets or cracks into the fire. These can explode when heated. Always be cautious when picking up rocks, as you may find unexpected guests like rattlesnakes or scorpions hiding underneath. Use a stick to flip rocks over first.

If you're stranded for more than a day or have some extra time, you can build a big fire in a trench the size of your body. Once it burns down to coals, cover the entire fire bed with sand or dirt. Put green branches on top, and you'll have a warm bed. These branches prevent you from accidentally exposing the coals while you sleep. Another way to make a heated bed is by building a fire on a large rock you plan to sleep on. After brushing off the coals, the rock stays warm for hours.

Remember to extinguish your campfire before leaving. Pour water on it if possible, and stir it with a stick to ensure it's out. If you don't have water, cover the fire with a thick layer of dirt or sand. Ensure the fire is entirely out before you go. This is vital because many forest and brush fires have started from campfires that weren't correctly extinguished and which smoldered for hours.

# Section 6: Water and Edibles

In this section, you will learn about the most essential items in bushcraft: water and edibles. You will discover their importance, how to find and identify them, and how to prepare these items safely. With these invaluable skills, you can survive almost anywhere!

## Why Is Water Vital for Survival?

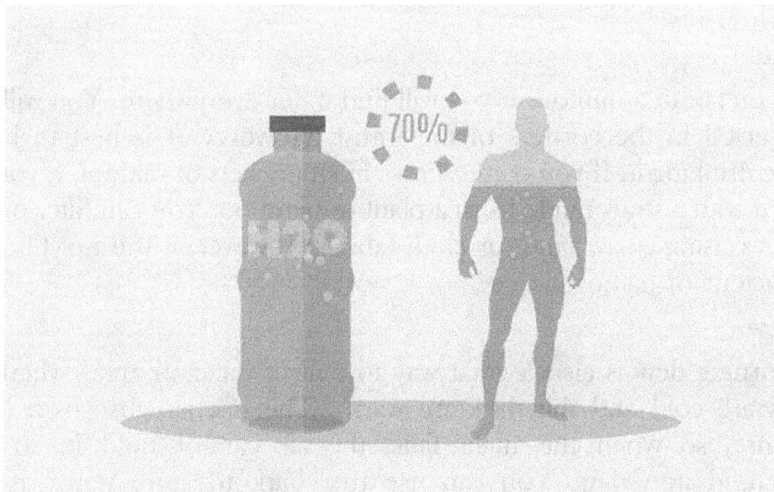

**You must always keep a water bottle with you or have a water source with you at all times.**
*https://pixabay.com/vectors/water-drink-body-human-hydration-5767178/*

Going without water for too long causes you to become seriously dehydrated, which can be fatal. You must always keep a water bottle with you or always have a water source with you. In hot, arid desert environments, the consequences of dehydration are much more serious than in milder environments. Even mild dehydration can negatively impact your mental and physical well-being, which may cause you to make poor decisions.

If you are in snowy surroundings, dehydration may not be a huge concern. You can always eat snow to hydrate yourself. However, you must be cautious, as eating too much snow can cause your core body temperature to drop. It should not be a problem if you are traveling or physically active. If your body temperature drops, you can always engage in physical activities like squats or jumping jacks. You must always try to melt snow if possible. If your body temperature drops below a certain level, you can become a victim of hypothermia. Here are some sources where you can find water in the wilderness:

### Gravity

Gravity is your friend when it comes to finding water in the wilderness. You must look for water in the lowest elevation areas, such as valleys. Usually, the water is drained and collected in the form of a pool. Even if there is no sign of water there, you can dig the ground to reveal some water that will gather in the hole you've dug. You may also find water in green areas with plants, as that is also a sign of the presence of water.

### Rain

If you are in a rainforest, you will find water everywhere. You will find it collected in the corners of the forest. However, it is best to boil it before drinking it. If you come across fresh pockets of rainwater, you can drink it with a straw made from a plant or bamboo. You can filter out big particles using grass, sand, or cloth fabric. However, it will not filter out the bacteria or pathogens.

### Dew

Morning dew is also a great way to collect water in areas where the nights are cold and the days are warm. The hot air absorbs a lot of moisture, so when the night falls, the air cannot hold it, so it is condensed into dew. You can use tree bark to store water as it is waterproof and does not absorb water. You can also use clothes to absorb the dew drops and wring them into the boiling pot. You can wrap these clothes around your legs and walk through the grass to absorb dew from the grass. You can then wring that water into a pot and boil it for safe consumption.

### Vegetation

If you are looking for water, it is always good to look around green vegetation. If you come across green foliage, you can know for certain that there is water there. Even if you don't see any water there, you can try digging the ground, and it will eventually cause water to come up. Moreover, a place with animals is another sign of the presence of water.

# Risks of Drinking Untreated Water

It is imperative to consume safe drinking water while you are on your outdoor adventure. However, in the absence of it, you must refrain from drinking unhealthy water. You must not drink directly from natural raw water sources, as it can be full of bacteria and viruses. There is a risk of getting dangerous waterborne viral diseases like rotavirus and hepatitis A. You can also feel nauseated and get stomach cramps and aches from drinking dirty water. Moreover, you can get parasites, worms, or diarrhea from drinking from these unhealthy sources. This is why you must boil water before consuming it.

# Water Purification Methods

Once you have sourced and collected your water, always purify it before consumption. There are many ways you can purify or filter your water in nature:

### Boiling

Boiling water is the safest and simplest way of making water safe for consumption.
*SMART Servier Medical Art, CC BY-SA 3.0 <https://creativecommons.org/licenses/by-sa/3.0>,
via Wikimedia Commons:
https://commons.wikimedia.org/wiki/File:Boiling_water_in_a_pan.png*

Boiling water is the safest and simplest way of making water safe for consumption. It eliminates all the bacteria and viruses but not chemicals. If you can access fire and wood, boil water before drinking it. You must boil water for a longer time if you're on elevation. You can boil water in a metal pot or nesting cup. Do not use insulated metal cups, or you will burn a hole in them.

### Coarse Filtration

You can filter water by coarse filtration using a brown bag, a bandana, or a cloth to remove deposits and turbidity. Coarse filtration reduces bacteria or viruses if attached to dirt but does not filter out the largest pathogenic organisms. This method to clean water is used before chemical methods to clean more efficiently.

### Microfiltration

Using pumps, ceramic filters, or gravity systems, you can employ microfiltration techniques to remove large pathogenic organisms, including protozoa, without using heat. However, it may not be effective for viruses and bacteria.

### Chemical Sterilization

Under adult supervision, you can also use chemical sterilization methods such as chlorine and iodine.

### Chlorine

Chlorine helps remove bacteria and viruses but does not get rid of protozoan cysts.

### Iodine

Iodine is excellent for cleaning turbid water and removing protozoa, bacteria, and viruses.

### Ultraviolet Techniques

You can use ultraviolet techniques to clean your water and remove bacteria, viruses, and protozoa. These devices, however, require the water to be filtered and clear. Also, these devices may require batteries.

# Wild Edibles

The world is filled with edibles. Wherever you go, there is a high chance you'll find edible plants around you, such as nuts, roots, berries, flowers, seeds, fungi, foliage, etc. Often, the whole plant is edible. Before you embark on your foraging journey, learn how to consume and identify plants. Do not eat anything that may seem edible. Certain toxic plants have a similar appearance to other plants. Keep a book or guide of edible plants with you to recognize the ones you can eat.

# General Rules for Foraging

Here are some general rules you must follow when foraging for food:

1. An animal eating it does not make the food safe for you to eat.
2. Do not consume a part of a plant without asking an adult.
3. If a plant is smelly, avoid it.
4. Poison ivy and other plants that grow in groups of three should not be eaten.
5. Plants that are found near busy roadsides or in developed regions should be thoroughly cleaned to prevent pollution from pesticides.
6. Not all plants are safe to be consumed raw.
7. Never consume rotting fruit or berries.
8. Ensure you are not allergic to a fruit, vegetable, or berry. Consume new plants slowly and one by one.
9. Wait a while before eating more so you know if there is any negative impact.
10. Always follow the Leave No Trace philosophy to ensure that your surroundings are pristine for the enjoyment of future visitors.

# Common Edible Plants

These plants are easy to identify and have at least one part you can consume safely. It is easy to locate these options throughout the United States. Pick up a local guide to identify and select your favorite wild food plants.

# 1. Nasturtium

**Look for nasturtium near your home before you embark on your outdoor adventure.**
*Sankar 1995, CC BY-SA 4.0 <https://creativecommons.org/licenses/by-sa/4.0>, via Wikimedia Commons: https://commons.wikimedia.org/wiki/File:Orange_Nasturtium_Flower_-_Shola_Gardens_-_Kotagiri.jpg*

Look for nasturtium near your home before you embark on your outdoor adventure. It's a lovely spicy plant that can be orange, yellow, or red. It can easily be found in gardens or parks and in the native land of South America. All parts of this plant, from seeds to leaves, are edible and rich in vitamins.

## 2. Prickly Pear Cactus

You can find food even in the desert. Mexico and the American Southwest are home to prickly pear cacti. Its arms are paddle-shaped, and it contains vivid pink fruit. Before eating it, you have to peel its skin and remove its spines. Its fruit is widely used to make fresh pink juice.

## 3. Morel

Delicious mushrooms that grow in the spring are called morels. Ensure you don't stumble onto a "false morel," which can trick the uninformed eye and is somewhat harmful.

## 4. Pine Nuts

Pine nuts are incredibly delicious and nourishing, but they need a lot of time to gather. This is why you must not consider them your go-to survival situation. These are seeds, not nuts, and are found in pinecones. The seeds of pinyon pines grow all over the American Southwest.

## 5. Dandelion

**Dandelions are edible and can be found everywhere.**
*Zeynel Cebeci, CC BY-SA 4.0 <https://creativecommons.org/licenses/by-sa/4.0>, via Wikimedia Commons: https://commons.wikimedia.org/wiki/File:Taraxacum_officinale_-_Common_dandelion_03.jpg*

Dandelions are edible and can be found everywhere. The leaves should be consumed young because they eventually turn bitter and include vitamins K and A. The mature leaves and roots must be cooked before eating for improved flavor. The golden blossom can be added to a salad or eaten raw.

# Plants to Avoid

You must learn how to identify edible plants from poisonous ones. Awareness of them will help you and your pets stay safe, as they can also be found in your backyard and parks.

### 1. Horse Nettle

The fruit of the horse nettle resembles cherry tomatoes because it is a member of the eggplant or tomato family. The fruit may seem appetizing but is toxic; therefore, you should not eat it. It is found in the American South. It consists of spines and tastes bitter.

## 2. Doll's Eyes

**These berries are white with black dots in the center.**

These berries are white with black dots in the center. They resemble a doll's eyes, hence the name. The whole plant is toxic and can be found in the eastern side of the US.

## 3. Poison Ivy

Humans cannot eat poison ivy even though birds eat its seeds and deer consume its leaves. It gives people an itchy rash, so learn to identify it as it grows in shrubs, fields, parks, and vines.

## 4. Oleander

**Oleander features lovely blossoms and smells delicious, like apricots.**

Oleander features lovely blossoms and smells delicious, like apricots. However, all parts of this plant are toxic and can kill you. They are found in Florida, Texas, and California.

### 5. Manchineel

Manchineel trees are extremely dangerous. Consuming its apple-like fruit can prove to be fatal. It is also called the tree of death. It is found in the Florida Keys and southern Florida. It grows wild along swampy or coastal locations in Central America, Mexico, and the Caribbean.

# How to Identify and Assess the Edibility of Wildlife

You should know how to identify and assess the edibility of wild animals and insects. You must always be under adult supervision while dealing with wild animals and learn about their species, habitats, and behaviors, especially those around the water source. Be aware of edible and non-edible animal parts. Furthermore, see if you can determine what illnesses an animal may have. Lastly, always respect nature and animals and avoid disturbing them.

# Cooking Methods and Preservation Techniques

Learning to cook and preserve food is a rewarding life skill that will help you become more self-reliant. Here are some cooking and preservation techniques.

### Cooking Techniques

### Campfire Cooking

You can build a campfire and use skewers for roasting marshmallows. You may also cook food like hot dogs, vegetables, and small pieces of meat over an open flame by putting it on sticks or skewers.

### Solar Cooking

You can use a solar oven to cook food. You can align the oven with the sun to cook things like smores.

## Boiling and Grilling

**Grilling can help you cook meat or vegetables over the flames.**

You can boil water to cook pasta, rice, and soup. Grilling can help you cook meat or vegetables over the flames.

### Preservation Techniques

### Drying

You can air dry your fruit and vegetables to avoid spoilage and also store them in containers to use in the future.

### Smoking

You can smoke your meat or fish to preserve it. Do it with an adult, as it can be complicated.

### Canning

You can prepare jams and pickles for canning. You need sterilized jars for proper sealing.

# Section 7: First Aid Basics

Imagine you're out in the wilderness, surrounded by towering trees, winding rivers, and the sounds of birds and insects. It's a thrilling adventure but can also be where things sometimes go differently than planned. That's why you need to know all about first aid, especially when there's no hospital nearby or when it might take time for medical assistance to arrive.

### Far from Help

Sometimes, you can be far from towns or cities when exploring the wild. Therefore, if something goes wrong, you may not be able to get to a hospital quickly. Knowing first aid means you can help yourself and your friends until the grown-ups arrive.

### Quick Thinking

When accidents happen, they don't wait. You must know what to do right away. First aid teaches you to think fast and act smart in emergencies, like when someone gets hurt or suddenly feels sick.

### Nature's Surprises

The wilderness is full of surprises – some are amazing, like spotting a deer, and some are a bit scary, like getting stung by a bee or tripping on a rock. First aid helps you handle these surprises, whether a small scratch or a bigger problem, like knowing what to do if you meet a wild animal.

### Be a Helper

When you know first aid, you can be a hero. If someone's hurt or in trouble, you can be the one to make things better. It feels great to help others and make sure they're safe.

### Safety with Friends

If you're out exploring with your friends, it's not just about keeping yourself safe - it's about keeping them safe, too. First aid skills help you care for your buddies and ensure everyone has a fun and safe adventure.

### Stopping Small Problems

Sometimes, a small problem can turn big if you need help figuring out what to do, but with first aid, you can stop minor problems from worsening. For example, if you get a cut, knowing how to clean and bandage it can stop it from getting infected.

So, learning first aid in the wilderness is more than just knowing how to put on a bandage. It's about preparing for the unexpected, helping others, and ensuring you have the best adventure ever. It's a life skill that keeps you and your friends safe while you explore the incredible world of nature.

# Accessing Injuries and Illnesses

### Step 1: Stay Calm

In any emergency, the first thing to do is to keep a clear and calm mind. Take a deep breath and try not to panic. This will help you think more clearly and make better decisions.

### Step 2: Check for Dangers

Before you approach anyone who needs help, take a good look around. Make sure the area is safe for you to enter to avoid making a bad situation worse. Check for slippery rocks, thorny bushes, or other potential hazards. If it's not safe, then don't go any further. Your safety is essential, too.

### Step 3: Assess the Situation

Approach the person who needs help, but do it carefully. If they're unconscious, gently shake their shoulders and talk to them. Ask loudly, "Are you okay?" If they don't respond, this is a severe situation. It's time to get help from an adult or call for assistance if you have a phone.

## Step 4: Ask Questions

**If the person is conscious and able to talk, ask them what happened.**

If the person is conscious and able to talk, ask them what happened. "Can you tell me what happened?" Listen carefully to their answers. It will give you essential information about their condition.

## Step 5: Look for Injuries

Carefully check the person's body for any injuries. Look for cuts, scrapes, bruises, or anything that looks unusual. When you find an injury, pay close attention. If there's bleeding, that's a top priority to take care of. Use a clean cloth or bandage to stop the bleeding and protect the area.

## Step 6: Check for Illness

Sometimes, people feel sick in the wilderness. They may have symptoms like dizziness, a headache, nausea, or extreme heat or cold. Ask them about how they're feeling and what they're experiencing. Look for signs like sweating, paleness, or redness of the face. These signs can give you clues about what might be wrong.

## Step 7: Prioritize Care

Now, you need to decide what needs your attention most urgently. Remember the three Ps: Preserve Life, Prevent Further Injury, and Promote Recovery.

**Preserve Life:** If someone is not breathing or their heart is not beating, you need to start CPR (if you know how) or get an adult to help immediately. This is the most critical because it's about saving their life.

**Prevent Further Injury:** If there is bleeding, apply pressure to stop it. If someone has a broken bone, try to keep it from moving. Ensure the person is safe from any other dangers present in the area.

**Promote Recovery:** After addressing immediate dangers, your next goal is to keep the person comfortable. For example, if they're cold, provide them with a blanket. If they're thirsty, offer water. If they have a headache, suggest they rest and take deep breaths.

### Step 8: Get Help

In severe situations, informing an adult and calling for help is crucial. If you have a phone, use it to call emergency services or get in touch with someone who can help. If there's no phone signal, send someone to find a park ranger or another responsible person nearby.

Remember, it's crucial to stay within your comfort zone. If the situation is too big or risky for you to handle, find an adult and let them take charge. Knowing how to assess injuries and illnesses in the wilderness is like becoming a real-life hero and nature detective. You gather clues, make wise decisions, and help those in need. These skills make your outdoor adventures safer and more enjoyable for everyone involved.

# First Aid Supplies to Include

A well-prepared bushcraft kit should include essential first aid supplies to address common wilderness injuries and ailments. Here's a list of basic first-aid supplies for your bushcraft kit:

### Adhesive Bandages

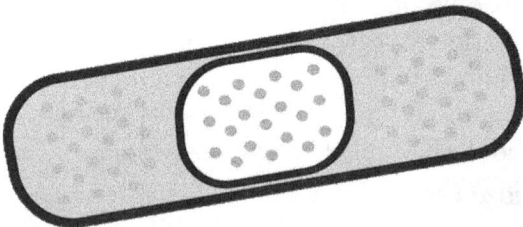

They are often called "band-aids," small, sticky strips with a padded center.
https://pixabay.com/vectors/band-aid-first-aid-medical-adhesive-3116999/

They are often called "band-aids," small, sticky strips with a padded center. They cover and protect small wounds like cuts, blisters, or abrasions. Different sizes are available to match the wound's dimensions and location.

### Sterile Gauze Pads

Gauze pads are made of sterile, woven fabric for dressing larger wounds, burns, or deep cuts. They keep the wound clean and help prevent infection. Gauze rolls are used to secure dressings in place, especially for wrapping or covering larger injuries.

### Medical Tape

Medical tape is a special adhesive tape designed for medical applications. It's used to secure gauze, bandages, or other dressings in place, ensuring they remain clean and firmly attached to the skin.

### Antiseptic Wipes or Solution

Wipes or solutions contain disinfectants for cleaning wounds and preventing infection. Wiping the area around a cut or scrape reduces the risk of harmful bacteria entering the wound, promoting faster healing.

### Scissors and Tweezers

Used for cutting medical tape, clothing, or bandages to the desired length. Tweezers are used for safely and accurately removing splinters, thorns, or other foreign objects from wounds without using your fingers, which may introduce infection.

### Elastic Bandage

Elastic bandages are stretchy and support sprained or strained limbs, such as ankles or wrists. They help reduce swelling and immobilize injured areas to prevent further damage.

### Pain Relievers

Acetaminophen or ibuprofen can alleviate minor discomfort caused by headaches, muscle aches, or minor pain from injuries. They can make a patient feel more comfortable.

### Antihistamine (for Allergic Reactions)

Antihistamines, often available as pills or creams, are used to manage allergic reactions, insect stings, or mild allergic symptoms. They work by reducing itching and swelling associated with allergies.

## Cotton Swabs

Cotton balls and swabs are versatile and can be used for various medical tasks, such as cleaning wounds, applying ointments or creams, or helping with hygiene in the field.

## Thermometer

A thermometer is a device for measuring body temperature. Elevated temperature can indicate fever or illness, essential to monitor in the wilderness.

## Tweezers

Tweezers are fine-tipped, precision instruments for safely removing splinters, thorns, or other foreign objects embedded in the skin. You must keep them clean and sterile.

## Emergency Blanket

An emergency blanket, or a space blanket, is a compact, lightweight, and reflective sheet that helps retain body heat. It can provide warmth and shelter in cases of exposure or shock.

## Tourniquet (for Severe Bleeding)

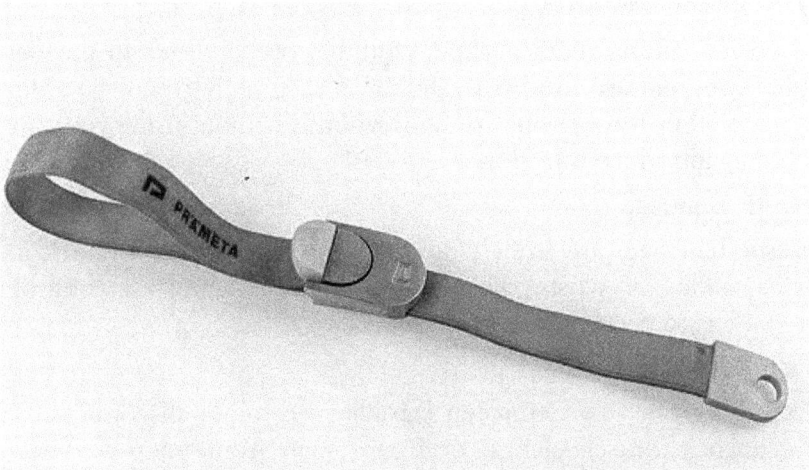

A tourniquet should be used only in extreme cases when other means cannot control severe bleeding.

A tourniquet should be used only in extreme cases when other means cannot control severe bleeding. Proper training is necessary to avoid complications when applying a tourniquet.

### Cleansing Soap or Hand Sanitizer

Proper hand hygiene prevents contamination of wounds and equipment. Use cleansing soap or hand sanitizer before treating injuries to reduce the risk of infection.

### First Aid Manual or Guide

A first-aid manual provides detailed instructions on administering first-aid in various situations. Have one with you in case you encounter unfamiliar injuries or medical issues.

### Emergency Contact Information

Include a list of emergency contacts, such as family members, friends, or park rangers. This information is vital if you or your group requires assistance in a wilderness emergency.

### Prescription Medications (If Necessary)

If you or someone in your group needs prescription medications for a medical condition, ensure these medications are included in your first aid kit.

Remember that your bushcraft first aid kit should be customized based on the specific needs of your adventure and the number of people in your group. Regularly check and replenish supplies as they are used or expired. Learning how to use these supplies effectively through first aid training or courses will benefit you in a wilderness setting.

# Wound Care

### Cuts and Scrapes

1. **Wash Hands:** First, wash your hands with soap and water.
2. **Clean the Wound:** Clean the cut or scrape with mild soap and water. Use a clean cloth or gauze.
3. **Stop Bleeding:** If it's bleeding, press a clean cloth or bandage firmly on the wound for a few minutes until the bleeding stops.
4. **Apply an Antiseptic:** Put some antiseptic on a cotton ball and gently apply it to the wound.
5. **Cover with a Bandage:** Place a band-aid or sterile gauze over the wound and use medical tape to keep it in place.

### Burns

1. **Cool the Burn:** Run cold water over the burn for about 10 minutes to cool it down. Don't use ice.

2. **Cover with Gauze:** Cover the burn with sterile gauze or a clean cloth after cooling.

3. **Elevate:** Keep it elevated to reduce swelling if it's an arm or leg burn.

4. **Don't Pop Blisters:** If you see blisters, don't pop them. They protect the burn.

### Sprains and Strains

1. **Rest:** Don't use it if you hurt a joint or muscle. Rest is crucial.

2. **Ice:** Put an ice pack (a cloth with ice inside) on the area for 15-20 minutes every hour.

3. **Compression:** Use an elastic bandage to wrap the injured area gently to reduce swelling.

4. **Elevate:** Raise the injured limb to heart level, like putting a pillow under your ankle.

### Bites and Stings

If you're stung by a bee, carefully scrape out the stinger with your fingernail or with a credit card.

1. **Wash with Soap:** Wash the bite or sting area with soap and water.

2. **Cold Pack:** Put a cold pack on the bite or sting to ease pain and swelling.

3. **Pain Reliever:** If it hurts, you can take a pain reliever as directed.

### Allergic Reactions

1. **Stay Calm:** If you have an allergy and start to feel bad, stay calm and tell an adult.

2. **Use an EpiPen:** If you have one, use an EpiPen as instructed. Ask an adult for help.

3. **Call 911:** Ask someone to call 911 right away for more help.

### Dehydration

1. **Drink Water:** When hot or sweating, drink water even if you're not thirsty.

2. **Rest in the Shade:** Find some shade to rest if you're feeling too hot.

3. **Cool Down:** Use a wet cloth on your face and neck to cool down.

## Hypothermia

1. **Warm Up**: If it's cold and you're shivering, get inside a shelter or put on dry, warm clothes.

2. **Cover Up**: Use a blanket or sleeping bag to stay warm.

## Basic CPR

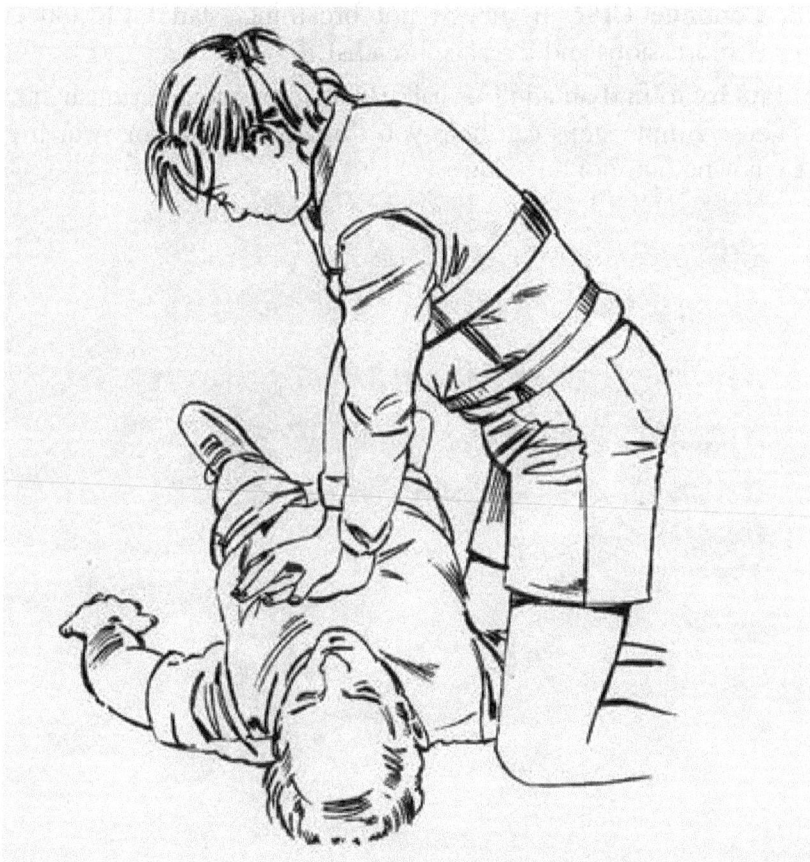

If you know how to, begin CPR (chest compressions and rescue breaths) until help arrives.
https://commons.wikimedia.org/wiki/File:Cardiopulmonary_Resuscitation_Adult.jpg

1. **Check for Breathing**: Tap the person and ask loudly, "Are you okay?" Check if they are breathing.

2. **Call for Help**: If they're not breathing, shout for an adult and call 911.

3. **Start CPR**: If you know how to, begin CPR (chest compressions and rescue breaths) until help arrives.

## Rescue Breathing

1. **Open the Airway:** Tilt the person's head back to open their airway.

2. **Breathe for Them:** Pinch their nose and give two rescue breaths, watching their chest rise.

3. **Continue CPR:** If they're not breathing, start CPR (30 chest compressions and 2 rescue breaths).

Always try to find an adult or call 911 if someone is seriously hurt or sick. These simple steps can help you care for yourself or your friends while enjoying outdoor adventures.

# Section 8: Food Finding Skills

Being capable of hunting, trapping, and gathering food in the wilderness will empower you and deepen your understanding of the natural world. These survival techniques are exciting and educational. You'll learn how to locate, catch, and harvest food from the wild, fostering resourcefulness and a deep connection with the environment. So, get ready to dive into the wilderness and discover these timeless skills that will stay with you forever.

## Knowing Local Flora and Fauna

You may wonder why getting to know the plants and animals in the area where you live is incredible. It's like having a natural wonderland at your doorstep, waiting to be explored and cherished. You get to discover how everything in your environment fits together and the species dominant in the surrounding habitat. Have you ever wondered how birds find food, where frogs like to hang out, or which plants you can eat safely? These are the questions that exploring your local flora and fauna can help you answer.

With exploration, you'll discover that many plants are more than just a way of nature to add foliage to the environment. Medicine in ancient times was all made of natural elements, including medicinal plants, having tons of health benefits. The more you explore, the more you understand about foraging the right foods. Imagine picking wild berries from a hiking trail in the mountains and consuming them because you know they're perfectly safe.

But it's not just about science and survival; it's also about connecting with your community's traditions. Different places have unique ways of doing things, and by exploring your local flora and fauna, you can learn about the traditions passed down through generations. Research the plants and animals in your area to get a clear perspective of the ecosystem surrounding you. You'll be amazed to know the plants you thought were useless have health-benefiting properties when foraged and consumed correctly.

Hunting and trapping are traditional methods of obtaining wildlife for food and other resources that have been practiced for centuries. However, in the modern world, certain regulations for hunting and trapping are categorized as illegal only to conserve the ecosystem and to promote animal welfare.

These techniques have evolved over time, and today, they encompass many methods and tools. Some methods are highly advanced and use modern equipment, while others are more primitive, relying on basic tools and skills. Here, you'll explore various hunting and trapping techniques, including both modern and primitive methods:

# Modern Hunting Techniques

**Firearms:** Firearms, such as rifles and shotguns, are the most common tools used for hunting today. They are accurate and powerful, allowing hunters to take down targets from a distance.

**Bowhunting:** Bowhunting involves using bows and arrows. Compound bows and crossbows are popular choices. This method requires a high skill level due to the need for accuracy and a short effective range.

**Black Powder Guns:** Muzzleloaders and other black powder firearms provide a more traditional hunting experience. They are slower to reload but offer a sense of history and challenge.

**Crossbows:** Crossbows are a modern variation of the bow and arrow, known for their accuracy and power. They are popular among hunters who appreciate the feel of traditional archery.

**Scouting:** Successful hunting often starts with scouting the area. Hunters look for signs of game, such as tracks, scat, and feeding areas. Understanding the terrain, vegetation, and local weather patterns is crucial.

# Primitive Hunting Techniques

**Snares:** Snares are simple yet effective primitive tools used for trapping animals. They consist of a looped cord or wire set along animal trails or paths. When an animal passes through, the snare tightens around its body, restraining it.

**Deadfalls:** Deadfalls are basic trapping devices where a heavy object is propped up, and when an animal triggers it, the weight falls and crushes or traps the animal.

**Cage Traps:** Cage traps are more humane and catch animals without harming them. Trappers then release the captured animal at a later time.

**Foot-Hold Traps:** Foot-hold traps are designed to restrain an animal's leg when it steps on the trap. This allows the trapper to approach and humanely dispatch the animal.

**Atlatl:** The atlatl is a primitive weapon for throwing spears with more force and accuracy. It extends the hunter's arm's length, providing a mechanical advantage.

**Blowgun:** Blowguns are a tool used for silently hunting small game and birds. The hunter blows through the tube to propel small darts, typically poisoned, toward the target.

Remember that hunting and trapping should always be conducted ethically and with respect for wildlife and local regulations. Sustainability and responsible practices protect both the environment and the animals you target. Additionally, if you plan to engage in these activities, consider taking courses or learning from experienced individuals to ensure safe and humane practices.

# Essential Fishing Skills

Wait for the fish to bite, then set the hook by quickly jerking the rod upwards when you feel a pull.

*https://www.pexels.com/photo/person-fishing-294674/*

## Angling

You'll need a fishing rod, reel, fishing line, and various hooks, baits, and lures for angling. Choose the appropriate gear for the type of fish you're targeting. Cast your line into the water, allowing your bait or lure to float, sink, or swim at various depths. Use different casting techniques, such as overhead casting or sidearm casting, depending on your target and surroundings.

Angling requires patience. Wait for the fish to bite, then set the hook by quickly jerking the rod upwards when you feel a pull. Once you've hooked a fish, play it by reeling it in and letting it tire itself out. Use the rod to control the fish's movements and prevent it from escaping.

### Setting Lines

**Limblines and Juglines**: These are passive fishing methods. Attach baited hooks to lines secured to floating objects like jugs or tree limbs. Submerge them in the water and check them periodically to see if you've caught any fish.

**Trotlines:** Trotlines are longer lines with multiple baited hooks. They are anchored in place and can be set overnight. Check them regularly to retrieve any caught fish.

### Fish Traps

**Hoop Nets:** Hoop nets are cylindrical nets with an entrance that leads to a baited central chamber. Fish swim in but have trouble finding their way out.

**Funnel Traps:** These traps have a funnel-like entrance that leads to a baited chamber. Once fish enter, it's challenging for them to exit.

### Spearfishing

Spearfishing requires a spear or pole with a sharp point, a mask, and a snorkel for underwater vision. A wetsuit will keep you warm and provide buoyancy. Approach fish carefully and patiently. Make a swift, accurate thrust with your spear when you get close.

### Ice Fishing

Ice fishing involves fishing through a hole in the ice. You'll need an ice auger, an ice fishing rod, and warm clothing to create the hole. Popular baits for ice fishing include worms, minnows, and jigs.

### Fly Fishing

Fly fishing uses a lightweight fly rod, reel, and specialized lines. The "flies" are often artificial lures made of feathers and other materials. Fly casting is a unique and graceful technique. You'll need to practice the art of casting to make the fly land gently on the water's surface.

### Using Fish Finders

Modern fish finders use sonar technology to locate fish in the water. Learn how to read the display to identify fish and their depth.

Remember to check local fishing regulations and obtain any required permits or licenses. Respect catch limits and practice catch-and-release when necessary to maintain healthy fish populations. Fishing is not just a skill; it's also an opportunity to connect with nature and enjoy the great outdoors.

# Tracking Skills

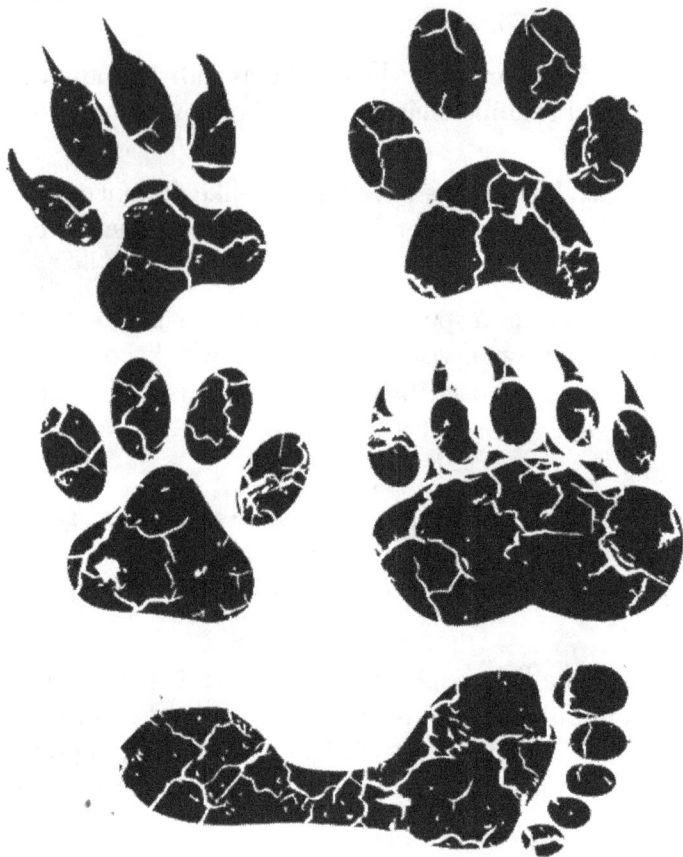

**Look for animal footprints in the mud, sand, or snow.**
*https://pixabay.com/vectors/paw-print-paw-foot-prints-footprint-2165814/*

**Animal Tracks:** Look for animal footprints in the mud, sand, or snow. These prints can tell you who passed by and when.

**Scat (Animal Droppings):** Yes, animal poop can tell you a lot! It can show you what animals eat and their size.

**Feeding Signs:** Check for nibbled plants or chewed tree bark. They're like breadcrumbs leading you to possible food sources.

**Prints and Trails:** Follow the trail of prints to see where an animal has been and where it might be headed.

## Observation Skills

**Silence and Patience:** Animals don't like noisy interruptions, so being quiet and patient helps you see them behaving naturally.

**Binoculars and Cameras:** Use binoculars or a camera to get a close-up view without scaring the animals.

**Field Guides:** Keep handy books to identify plants and animals in your area.

**Listening:** Pay attention to the sounds around you. Birds chirping or leaves rustling could reveal hidden animals.

By learning tracking and observation skills, you become a wildlife detective, discovering the secrets of nature. These skills will help you understand the natural world and make your outdoor adventures more exciting.

# Tips for Hunting

### Stalking Techniques

Move quietly and cautiously, keeping a low profile. Slow and deliberate movements are key to avoiding startling game animals. Take advantage of natural cover like rocks, trees, and bushes. Use them to break up your silhouette and hide from the sight of your prey. Pay attention to the wind. Keep it in your face so your scent is carried away from the animals you're pursuing. Animals rely heavily on their sense of smell. Avoid making unnecessary noise, such as stepping on dry leaves or snapping twigs. Walk softly and tread carefully.

### Camouflage

Choose camouflage clothing that matches the environment you're hunting in. This helps you blend into the surroundings. Camouflage your face and hands with paint or a mask to reduce the chance of being spotted. Equip yourself with camouflage gear, including hats, gloves, and even a backpack.

### Knowledge of Game Behavior

You must understand the habits and behavior of the game animals you're hunting. Study their feeding patterns, mating rituals, and preferred habitats. Hunt when your target species is most active, typically during dawn and dusk. Many animals are more active during these low-light periods. Learn to use game calls or decoys to attract or call in animals. This can be especially effective for species like waterfowl or turkeys.

### Scouting

Before the hunt, scout the hunting area to identify game trails, feeding areas, and bedding sites. Place trail cameras to capture images of wildlife activity in the area. This helps you learn about game movement and timing.

### Safety and Preparation

Prioritize safety by always following firearm safety rules and wearing appropriate safety gear, such as blaze orange clothing, to be visible to other hunters. Regular target practice and familiarity with your weapon will ensure accurate shooting.

### Patience

Hunting requires a great deal of patience. Stay still and quiet for extended periods while waiting for your opportunity.

### Ethical Considerations

Practice selective harvesting by targeting mature animals for a healthy and sustainable wildlife population. Respect wildlife by taking only ethical shots and ensuring quick, humane kills.

Remember that hunting should always be conducted ethically and under local hunting laws and regulations. A successful hunt is about bagging games, enjoying the outdoors, and respecting the natural world.

# Cooking Food Safely

Safe cooking methods and proper food handling practices in the wilderness prevent foodborne illnesses and ensure a safe outdoor adventure. Here are some necessary guidelines.

# Safe Cooking Methods

### Cooking Over a Fire

- Use a campfire or portable camp stove for cooking. Make sure the fire is completely extinguished after use.
- Control the heat by adjusting the distance between your cookware and the flames.
- Use a meat thermometer to ensure that meat is cooked to a safe temperature (e.g., poultry to 165°F or 74°C, and ground meat to 160°F or 71°C).

### Boiling Water

- Boiling water for at least one minute is one of the most effective ways to purify it, making it safe for cooking or drinking.

- Carry a reliable water purification system, such as water filters or purification tablets, if you need clarification on the water source's safety.

## Use Clean Utensils

- Clean cooking utensils and cookware by scrubbing them with biodegradable soap and water. Rinse thoroughly.
- Avoid cross-contamination by using separate cutting boards and utensils for raw and cooked food.

# Food Handling Practices

## Hand Hygiene

- Wash your hands with soap and clean water before handling food, especially after using the restroom or handling raw meat.
- Carry hand sanitizer for situations where water and soap are unavailable.

## Food Storage

- Use airtight, animal-resistant containers or bear canisters to store food. Hang food in bear bags if required in bear-prone areas.
- Keep perishable food in a cooler with ice packs to maintain safe temperatures.

## Food Separation

- Keep raw meat, poultry, and seafood separate from other foods to prevent cross-contamination.
- Use sealed plastic bags or containers to prevent juices from raw meat from leaking onto other items in your backpack.

## Clean Preparation Surfaces

- Use a clean, flat surface to prepare food. You can use a portable cutting board or a clean, flat rock.
- Avoid using surfaces that animals or chemicals may have contaminated.

## Food Inspection

- Inspect all food for signs of spoilage or damage before consuming it.
- Discard any canned food with visible dents, leaks, or bulges.

## Safe Water Sources

- Always use purified or boiled water for food preparation.

- Avoid using water from sources that may be contaminated, such as stagnant pools or water downstream from human activity.

## Cooling Leftovers

- Rapidly cool leftovers to safe temperatures (below 40°F or 4°C) and store them in a cooler.

- Reheat leftovers to a high temperature before consuming.

## Waste Disposal

- Dispose of food waste properly by packing it out in sealed bags. Leaving food scraps in the wilderness can attract wildlife.

Practicing safe cooking methods and food handling practices in the wilderness is crucial to prevent foodborne illnesses and maintain a healthy and enjoyable outdoor experience. Always follow Leave No Trace principles and local regulations for food storage and waste disposal in natural areas.

# Section 9: Extra Bushcraft Skills and Tips

This final section provides additional skills, tips, and hacks for safe and effective bushcraft practices. They're designed to take you from being proficient in fundamental skills to becoming more advanced practitioners who can handle various scenarios and challenges in the wilderness.

## Advanced Survival Skills

### Signaling

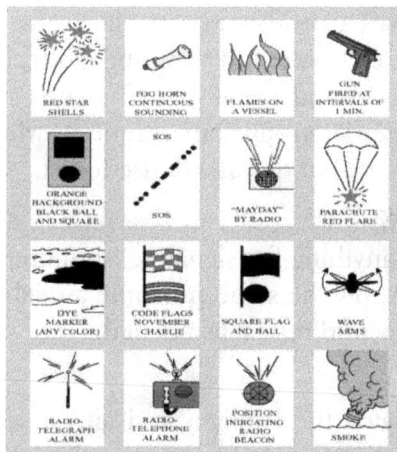

**Knowing distress signals and communication methods can be a lifesaver in the wilderness.**

https://commons.wikimedia.org/wiki/File:Distress_Signals.png

Knowing distress signals and communication methods can be a lifesaver in the wilderness. If you do not have access to a radio or a phone, your hands, a piece of cloth, smoke, and other items will be useful. For example, using a whistle (a highly recommended item for your gear list for outdoor adventures) is a great way to signal distress or alert wildlife of your presence.

### Whistle or Flashlight

A whistle blow is an unusual sound in the wild, and using it three times is a sure way to make others understand you need help. After each blow, pause for two seconds and then repeat. If there is anyone nearby, they'll pause and listen. Repeat the three-blow method several times to ensure you've been heard. You can use the same method using a flashlight during the night. Flash it (holding it straight ahead of you or slightly upward), turn it off, flash it again, and repeat.

### Smoke

Smoke signals are a great alternative during the day. You can make a fire or use smoke from the fire you used to cook, clean, etc. You'll need a dense smoke, so add grass and other greenery. Cover the fire you aren't using for other purposes with a wet cloth when the smoke gets dense. Keep the cover on for a few seconds, then remove it to let the smoke travel upwards. After a few seconds, put the cloth back on and repeat the previous steps as needed.

### Using Cloth

Because they stand out from the natural environment, brightly-colored clothing pieces can also be an alternative for creating visible signals. To signal distress, hold and wave the cloth above your head. Tie the cloth higher up around your camping area/shelter to alert wild animals. This will work in an environment where the colors are noticeable from far away, but not in a dense forest.

### Shouting or Yelling

If you don't have anything for signaling, shouting or yelling at regular intervals helps, too. Apply the same principle as with other methods. Let out a loud sound, stop, and repeat as needed.

### Mirrors

Tilt a mirror to catch the sunlight and aim it so the reflection goes upwards, making it easier for rescuers to see. Use this method the same way you would a whistle. Send a reflection signal for a second or two, cover it, and repeat it two more times. Wait a few seconds, then send another three signals, and repeat for as long as necessary.

### Wildlife Awareness Skills

Before you embark on an outdoor adventure, learn about local wildlife and their behavior. Do you know what animals live there and where they live? Do you know what they eat and how they act when feeling threatened? If not, look it up. It will help you understand the dangers you'll face in that specific area so you can adequately prepare for them.

Besides using them as food, you'll should the wildlife. This ensures your safety and is also for the animals' well-being. Respect their space and only observe them from a safe distance. If you encounter them unexpectedly, remain calm and don't approach them. Start backing away from them and leave them room so they can do the same. If they become aggressive, don't move but start making a noise. When traveling to a new area, make noises to alert them of your presence and avoid scaring them. Beyond storing your food items securely (ideally in canisters you can hang up and away from your sleeping area), it's also a good idea to dispose of your water and food remnants safely. Leaving a trace would attract animals.

### Identification Skills

Beyond identifying the tracks of animals you may want to hunt and poisonous plants to avoid foraging mishaps, you'll need other identification skills like knowing how to pick wood for different purposes. For example, softwoods like pine work better for starting a fire, whereas hardwoods are more durable and can be used for building a shelter or sustaining a fire for a long time.

### Prepping and Storing Skills

Knowing how to properly prepare your food will enable you to store it safely. Understanding *how to store it* will help you conceal it from wild animals so you don't attract them. However, choosing storage space for your food can be challenging in the wilderness. Beyond hanging it up, ensure the food is kept in a dry and cool place as well. Hang your food in a sealed container in the shade (where the temperatures don't go above 90 degrees in the summer and 30 in winter). Be aware of the pests and keep them away from your food and water.

## Using Glue

Packing light is essential when going on an outdoor adventure, and you might have only one of each storage item, like a water bottle. What happens if your trusty water bottle cracks? What if your tent gets damaged by the weather? These are classic situations when knowing how to use glue (a strong one, not the kind you use for school projects) will be handy.

Here are a few tips for using glue:

- Practice (under adult supervision at first) using different materials and strong adhesives.
- Put pressure on the glued item and look for cracks and fissures to determine whether the bond will hold.
- If you glue an item that's been glued before on the same place or which has an uneven surface, you'll need to sand the surface first to make the glue bond.
- Apply strong glues with their applicator or an item at hand (a piece of cloth, for example) and never with your hands.
- Clamp the two surfaces to create a stronger bond and make the process go faster.
- Read the adhesive guidelines regarding curing and drying times (the label should say when it is dry to the touch and when you can use the item safely).
- Learn what glue works best for what material (regardless of the label, some adhesives work better with some materials than others).

Alternatively, you can make glue from materials you find in the wilderness, like tree sap, resin, wax, bark, or honey. Look for sap or resin near wounded pine, fir, or spruce trees. You can also use willow and birch bark. Liquid material like sap can be used immediately after extracting it from the tree by cutting slightly into the place where you see the liquid coming out from a wound. If you're using hard material like resin or bark, chop it up into tiny pieces, mix it with water (1 part plant material, 2 parts water), bring to a boil in a pot, and cook it over a slow fire until it thickens (about 30 minutes).

# Additional Bushcraft Tips

## Keeping Yourself Entertained

If you're used to entertaining yourself with gadgets or hanging out with friends in a busy urban area, you'll be surprised how bored you'll get in the wilderness. It's quiet, and if you're out with a larger group, all tasks will be done in no time, so you'll have plenty of time on your hands. The good news is that keeping yourself entertained is a skill you can learn through *practice*. Moreover, the bigger your group is, the greater the chances that someone will devise a plan for engaging everyone and making your adventure a fun experience. Think about what you could do that doesn't involve electronics or making loud noises. Games that don't require much gear and lookout schedules (for animals and plants you've previously read about) are great options.

### Make Practice Fun

Everything is easier to learn if you make practicing it fun. For example, you can turn the practice of identifying stones into something more, like a rock-throwing contest. When looking for firewood, you could list other purposes for what you've gathered (like making a shelter, using a sharp stick for spearing fish, etc.)

### Work on Your Awareness

Moving with stealth, patience, and situation awareness are two crucial skills you'll need in the wilderness. On the one hand, you'll need to move in such a way as to make as little noise as possible. On the other hand, you must know when to stop and listen out for signs of wildlife. It will also teach you how to wait patiently and in silence. You can practice this by listening to how others move through the house or outdoors when no other noises are around.

### Get Used to Sleeping in Unusual Places

If you're used to sleeping in a dark room in a comfortable bed, out in nature, every little sound or sign of discomfort will wake you up. You can make your shelter as comfortable as possible by using the right materials - but you'll still need to learn how to sleep with nature's sounds and being a little uncomfortable (like if you're sleeping area is a bit warmer than usual or when you don't have as much room as you're used to having in your bed). Sleeping better will help you be more alert during the day to avoid mistakes and injuries.

## Practice Often

Everyone learns at different speeds based on their interests, supplies, abilities, and opportunities. This is entirely normal. Don't be discouraged if you can't master a skill immediately. Everyone makes mistakes when learning something. Practice makes perfect, and some skills take longer to learn than others. Start with the basics and practice them as often as possible. Only move on to advanced skills when you're confident with the basics. Practicing repeatedly will also enable you to learn from your mistakes much sooner.

Practice even those bushcraft skills you are good at so you won't get out of practice. Some skills are easier to remember, while others aren't. If you don't practice the skills you've already mastered, you could fail to get them right in an emergency situation or when you're feeling tired after a long day spent outdoors.

## Learn to Work with Others

While exploring nature with a group can be fun, there will be times when not everyone will get along. You might disagree on how something should be done. However, for everyone's safety, you must learn how to work with others even if you don't get along with them or disagree with their opinion. Sometimes you just have to compromise.

Another issue that might arise is the feeling that not everyone does their share of the workload. For example, you may get upset because one person refused to clean up while others went for supplies and cooked. Instead of getting angry, ask them why they didn't clean up and listen to their side regardless of your feelings. After listening to them, explain why you think their behavior is unfair and try to reach a compromise.

You should also listen to what others say when you disagree on doing something. Listening to them will help you understand why they want to do it the way they do, and you'll be able to decide whether you disagree. Showing you care about other people's opinions is necessary for good teamwork. It builds camaraderie and ensures everyone will know to count on others to survive and thrive in the wild.

## Practice Relaxing

While staying alert is needed many times in the wilderness, being in this state will make you anxious and stressed. It will cause you to sleep poorly and overreact to every little noise or sight that appears suddenly. Sometimes, you need to relax and let others (and your gear and protective measures) keep you safe.

**Think before You Act**

The wilderness can be unpredictable, but with good preparation, you can predict and learn what to do in every circumstance. If you find yourself in a situation where you don't know what will happen next, take a moment to think. Your action can make a difference in staying safe or walking into a dangerous situation like encountering wild animals or finding yourself in a terrain full of hidden perils. Think about where you are and what dangers could lie ahead in your current location. In the beginning, this will be a challenging skill to master, but it will become much easier with practice.

# Thank You Message

Thank you for choosing and reading this book. By the end of the book, you've become richer with a broad range of skills and knowledge about how to survive in the wild. You've learned what gear you need for bushcraft, how to secure knots, build a shelter and a fire, find water and food resources, and what to do if someone gets hurt or ill. Spending time in nature can be a scary prospect. However, now that you have acquired all these skills, you have nothing to fear anymore because you will know what to do in every situation. Although it's always advisable to explore the outdoors in the company of adults, having some bushcraft tricks up your sleeves will help you become more independent during your adventures.

Now, it is time to put your knowledge into practice as you continue learning about bushcraft. Remember, this is a complex set of skills that takes time, dedication, and patience to master. Besides, the more bushcraft talents you master, the higher your chances of survival should you find yourself without help in the wilderness.

You can help organize your next adventure and showcase your newly acquired skills only on your journey. Taking the initiative and actively keeping yourself and others safe in your outdoor explorations will further empower you with much-needed practical experience. As you do, you can use this book as a stepping stone and a reference for your future learning about bushcraft and wilderness survival.

Practicing what you learned from this book will make you more confident in your practical outdoor skills. As you apply these talents, you'll see just how many adventures the great outdoors holds. At times, it will teach you how to be more independent and think outside the box, while in other circumstances, it will give you a chance to admire the natural beauties you can only see in the wilderness. Once again, thank you, and congratulations on completing this book and embarking on your very first bushcraft journey.

# Here's another book by Dion Rosser that you might like

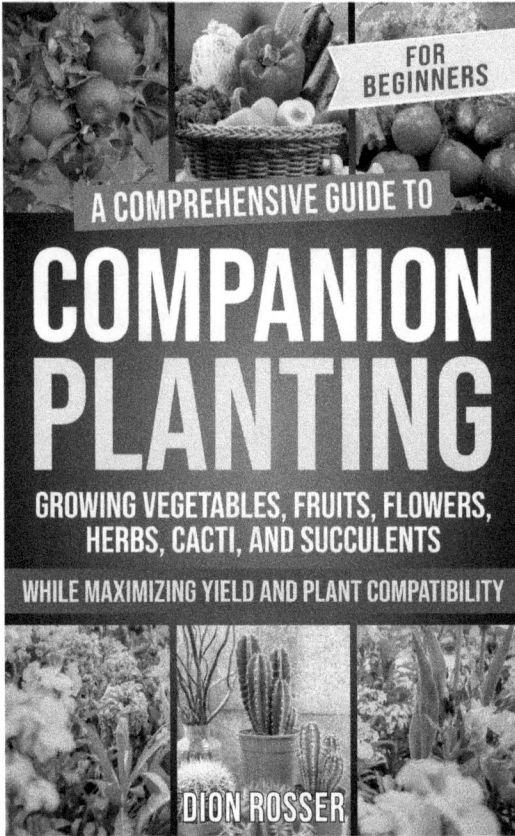

**FOR BEGINNERS**

A COMPREHENSIVE GUIDE TO

# COMPANION PLANTING

GROWING VEGETABLES, FRUITS, FLOWERS, HERBS, CACTI, AND SUCCULENTS

WHILE MAXIMIZING YIELD AND PLANT COMPATIBILITY

DION ROSSER

# References

10 essential outdoor survival tips. (n.d.). Nuvancehealth.Org. https://www.nuvancehealth.org/health-tips-and-news/10-essential-outdoor-survival-tips

3 Things You MUST Teach Children for Wilderness Survival. (n.d.). Survivalfitnessplan.Com. https://www.survivalfitnessplan.com/blog/wilderness-survival-lessons-children

Basic Knots. (2019, January 11). Animatedknots.com. https://www.animatedknots.com/basic-knots

Biggers, S. (2019, October 19). The Adhesives and Glues Every Prepper Needs. Backdoor Survival. https://www.backdoorsurvival.com/the-adhesives-and-glues-every-prepper-needs/

Biggers, S. (2020, April 8). Survival Skills List: 75 Important Skills From Basic To Advanced. Backdoor Survival. https://www.backdoorsurvival.com/survival-skills/

Brown, T., & Morgan, A. B., Jr. (2023, April 4). Making cordage from natural materials. Mother Earth News – The Original Guide To Living Wisely; Mother Earth News. https://www.motherearthnews.com/diy/making-cordage-natural-materials-zmaz83jfzraw/

Bushcraft basics - the ultimate beginners' guide - HANWAG STORIES. (2023, March 31).

Chowdhury, M. R. (2023, October 13). The positive effects of nature on your mental wellbeing. PositivePsychology.com. https://positivepsychology.com/positive-effects-of-nature/

Dale, A. (n.d.). What are the Essential Wilderness Skills? Tech Writer EDC. https://techwriteredc.com/the-art-of-survival-mastering-the-essential-skills-for-thriving-in-the-wilderness/

Dedman, G. (2019, December 2). 12 Essential items people should have with them when they venture outdoors. Bushcraft Survival Australia. https://bushcraftsurvivalaustralia.com.au/12-essential-items-people-should-have-with-them-when-they-venture-outdoors/

Dedman, G. (2021, January 31). Cordage - something you should never be without. Bushcraft Survival Australia. https://bushcraftsurvivalaustralia.com.au/cordage-something-you-should-never-be-without/

Dedman, G. (2022, August 10). Water acquisition and purification. Bushcraft Survival Australia. https://bushcraftsurvivalaustralia.com.au/water-acquisition-and-purification/

DeRushie, N. (2020). Fire and cooking. Woodland Bushcraft. https://www.woodlandbushcraft.com/fireandcooking

End, S. A. (2022, January 22). How to build a survival shelter in the wild. Survive After End. https://surviveafterend.com/how-to-build-a-survival-shelter-in-the-wild/

Environment, & Climate Change. (n.d.). Trapping and harvesting - kids and teachers. Gov.Nt.Ca. https://www.gov.nt.ca/ecc/en/services/trapping-and-harvesting/trapping-and-harvesting-kids-and-teachers

Fire Craft 101. (n.d.). Slideshare.net. https://www.slideshare.net/kevinestela/fire-craft-101-presentation

Foraging for beginners: Tips for safely gathering wild, edible foods. Waterproof, Windproof & Breathable Clothing. (2017, November 8). https://www.gore-tex.com/blog/foraging-food-wild-plants

FutureLearn. (2023, June 9). The importance of first aid: 5 reasons to learn. FutureLearn. https://www.futurelearn.com/info/blog/the-importance-of-learning-first-aid-5-reasons-to-learn

FutureLearn. (2023, June 9). The importance of first aid: 5 reasons to learn. FutureLearn. https://www.futurelearn.com/info/blog/the-importance-of-learning-first-aid-5-reasons-to-learn

Gebhardt, M. (n.d.). Outdoor skills: Meaning, definition, origin. Survival Kompass. https://survival-kompass.de/dictionary/outdoor-skills/

Graham, S. (2023, May 5). How to Make Glue in the Wild: A Comprehensive Guide. Glue Savior. https://gluesavior.com/how-to-make-glue-in-the-wild/

Handling food safely while eating outdoors. (2022, February 17). U.S. Food and Drug Administration; FDA. https://www.fda.gov/food/buy-store-serve-safe-food/handling-food-safely-while-eating-outdoors

Harbour, S. (2020, December 15). Wilderness survival kits for kids: What to include? An Off Grid Life. https://www.anoffgridlife.com/wilderness-survival-kits-for-kids/

How to choose a wilderness campsite. (n.d.). Wilderness.net. https://wilderness.net/learn-about-wilderness/benefits/outdoor-recreation/camping/where-to-camp.php

How to tie a bowline knot. (n.d.). Rmg.co.uk. https://www.rmg.co.uk/stories/topics/how-tie-bowline-knot

Hurley, T. (2011, March 17). Outdoor cooking safety. LoveToKnow. https://www.lovetoknow.com/food-drink/meal-ideas/outdoor-cooking-safety

Hypothermia. (n.d.). WebMD. https://www.webmd.com/a-to-z-guides/what-is-hypothermia

James, J. (2020, March 17). 7 best ropes for survival based on uses and situation. Survival Freedom; Jim James. https://survivalfreedom.com/7-best-ropes-for-survival-based-on-uses-and-situation/

Leave no trace. (2023, September 6). The 7 principles - leave no trace center for outdoor ethics. Leave No Trace. https://lnt.org/why/7-principles/

Life, T. M. O. (2020, July 1). Nine natural shelters that can save your life in the wild. Popular Science. https://www.popsci.com/story/diy/natural-shelters-save-life-wild/

MacWelch, T. (2013, February 21). Survival skills: How to scout a good campsite. Outdoor Life. https://www.outdoorlife.com/blogs/survivalist/2013/02/survival-skills-how-scout-good-campsite/

MacWelch, T. (2020, October 12). How to process and use animal sinew. Outdoor Life. https://www.outdoorlife.com/story/survival/how-to-process-and-use-animal-sinew/

Nalanda. (2023, September 26). How to plan your first outdoor adventure as a family with kids. Medium. https://medium.com/digital-global-traveler/how-to-plan-your-first-outdoor-adventure-as-a-family-with-kids-1bbaa961eb70

Nesbitt, E. (2023, September 8). The benefits of teaching your kids bushcraft and survival skills. Wildlings Forest School. https://www.wildlingsforestschool.com/blog/bushcraft-and-survival-life-skills

Off The Grid. (2010, September 7). Staying warm in an emergency - Insulation. Off Grid Survival - Wilderness & Urban Survival Skills. https://offgridsurvival.com/emergencyinsulation/

Onbekend, T. (n.d.). Knowing survival firecraft can save your life. Extopian. https://extopian.com/outdoors/knowing-survival-fire-craft-can-save-your-life/

Owen, R. (2016, July 18). Camping in unfavorable weather: What to pack. The National Wildlife Federation Blog. https://blog.nwf.org/2016/06/camping-in-unfavorable-weather-what-to-pack/

Poffe, B. (2015, May 22). Bushcraft family, reconnect with nature. Rewilding Drum België; Rewilding Drum. https://www.rewildingdrum.be/bushcraft-good-for-your-tribe-good-for-you/

Rejba, A. (2019, July 1). Why is Shelter Needed for Survival? The Smart Survivalist Blog. https://www.thesmartsurvivalist.com/why-is-shelter-needed-for-survival/

Safety Kits Plus. (2021, May 21). First Aid Kits For Hiking & adventures. Safety Kits Plus. https://www.safetykitsplus.com/blogs/safety/first-aid-kits-for-hiking

Safety Kits Plus. (2021, May 21). First Aid Kits For Hiking & adventures. Safety Kits Plus. https://www.safetykitsplus.com/blogs/safety/first-aid-kits-for-hiking

Sherpa, S. (n.d.). Fire craft skills –. Survival Sherpa. https://survivalsherpa.wordpress.com/tag/fire-craft-skills/

Spera, J. (2018, May 8). Camping gear: 27 essentials for camping with kids. Today's Parent: SJC Media. https://www.todaysparent.com/family/activities/camping-gear-essentials-kids/

Spirit, B. (n.d.). Survival basics. Survival Basics | Bushcraft Spirit. https://www.bushcraftspirit.com/survival-basics/

Stricklin, T. (2023, October 5). 15 dangerous diseases caused by contaminated drinking water. SpringWell Water Filtration Systems. https://www.springwellwater.com/15-dangerous-diseases-caused-by-contaminated-drinking-water/

Survival hunting and trapping. (2015, September 14). Survival Skills and Bushcraft for the Modern Survivalist. https://yostsurvivalskills.com/survival-hunting-trapping/

Survival, A. (n.d.). Fire Craft. Armstrong Survival. https://armstrongsurvival.com/tag/fire-craft/

Tautline hitch. (n.d.). Netknots.com. https://www.netknots.com/rope_knots/tautline-hitch

Teaching basic first aid to kids. (2020, December 14). RUN WILD MY CHILD. https://runwildmychild.com/teaching-first-aid/

Teaching basic first aid to kids. (2020, December 14). RUN WILD MY CHILD. https://runwildmychild.com/teaching-first-aid/

Teaching CPR to children. (2019, March 15). HSI. https://hsi.com/solutions/cpr-aed-first-aid-training/resources-media/blog/teaching-cpr-to-children

Teaching CPR to children. (2019, March 15). HSI. https://hsi.com/solutions/cpr-aed-first-aid-training/resources-media/blog/teaching-cpr-to-children

What's the best material to use for waterproofing a survival shelter? (2019, January 12). Bushcraft Buddy. https://bushcraftbuddy.com/whats-the-best-material-to-use-for-waterproofing-a-survival-shelter/

Wilderness survival shelter. (n.d.). Bushcraftspirit.com. http://www.bushcraftspirit.com/wilderness-survival-shelter/

Wilderness survival: Fire & Knives. (n.d.). Trackerspdx.com. https://trackerspdx.com/youth/halloween-camps/wilderness-survival-fall-fire-knives.php

Wilderness Survival: Firecraft. (n.d.). Wilderness-survival.net. https://www.wilderness-survival.net/chp7.php

Wilderness survival. (n.d.). Mountainshepherd.com. https://mountainshepherd.com/home-2/wilderness-survival/

Williams, T. (2023, June 27). How to build a shelter: Your home away from home. Desert Island Survival. https://www.desertislandsurvival.com/how-to-build-a-shelter/

Willis, D. (n.d.). What is Bushcraft? Bushcraft with David Willis. http://www.davidwillis.info/what-is-bushcraft